Mastering the Art of Homemade Pasta

Secrets of Delicious Fresh Pasta from Italy with Your Own Hands

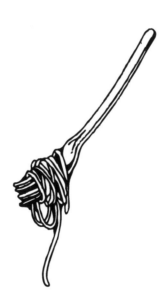

William Hunt

CONTENTS

INTRODUCTION

INTRODUCTION

There is something truly special about the taste and comfort of a warm bowl of homemade pasta. Whether you are enjoying a classic spaghetti carbonara or trying something new and innovative, there is no denying the simple pleasures of this timeless dish.

In this special book, we will dig deep into the world of pasta, exploring the different shapes, forms, and ingredients that make this dish so beloved. From recipes for classic pasta dishes to new and exciting creations, you will find everything you need to make your own delicious homemade pasta.

Mastering the Art of Homemade Pasta is a comprehensive guide to the culinary art of pasta making. With the popularity of Italian cuisine continuing to grow, there is an increasing interest in learning how to make pasta from scratch. This book is written for anyone who wants to explore the traditional techniques and ingredients that make homemade pasta a staple in Italian cuisine.

We will also take a closer look at the art of pasta and wine pairing, as well as tips on how to freeze and store your pasta for later. Whether you are a seasoned cook or just starting out, you will find the recipes and information in this book to be both accessible and inspiring. With step-by-step instructions and helpful tips, Mastering the Art of Homemade Pasta will guide you on your journey to becoming a pasta making expert.

Making pasta from scratch is a rewarding and fulfilling experience that requires a few basic ingredients and a lot of patience and love. The process of kneading the dough, rolling it out, and cutting it into various shapes can be therapeutic and result in a truly authentic taste.

So grab your apron, gather your ingredients, and prepare your mind to dive into the spectacular world of homemade pasta with me. Let's rediscover the joys of homemade pasta and bring a taste of Italy into your own kitchen.

Brief History of Pasta

1. Origin of Pasta

The exact origin of pasta is shrouded in mystery, with different theories tracing its roots to ancient civilizations like the Chinese and the Arabs. However, it is widely believed that pasta as known in today's world was first discovered in Italy in the thirteenth century. The dish quickly became a staple in Italian cuisine, with different regions developing their own unique pasta shapes and sauces.

2. Evolution of Pasta

Pasta has evolved over the centuries, with new shapes, flavors, and ingredients being added to the dish. During the Renaissance, pasta was considered a luxury food and was often served in the homes of the wealthy. In the nineteenth and twentieth centuries, advances in food processing and manufacturing allowed pasta to become more widely available, and it soon became a staple in households around the world.

3. Pasta in the American Market

Italian immigrants brought pasta to America in the late nineteenth and early twentieth centuries, and it swiftly established itself as a staple in American cuisine.Today, pasta is a multi-billion-dollar industry, with hundreds of different shapes, flavors, and brands available on the market. From classic spaghetti and meatballs to more innovative dishes like spaghetti carbonara and creamy fettuccine, pasta continues to be one of the most popular and beloved foods in the world.

Brief History of Pasta

1. Health Benefits

Making pasta at home allows you to control the ingredients, ensuring that you are using high-quality, nutritious ingredients. Homemade pasta is typically lower in sodium, saturated fat, and additives compared to store-bought pasta, and it can be made with healthier alternatives like whole grain flour and egg substitutes. By making your own pasta, you can create a unique dish that is both yummy and nutritious.

2. Cost Benefits

Making pasta at home is also cost-effective, especially when compared to the price of store-bought pasta. You can create a huge quantity of pasta using only a few simple components for a lot less money than it would cost to purchase pre-made pasta from the supermarket. This will assist you in saving lots of money as well as reduce food waste, as you can freeze and store your pasta for later use.

3. Flavor Benefits

Finally, making pasta at home allows you to create a dish that is truly your own. You can experiment with different flours, shapes, and sauces to create a pasta dish that is unique to your tastes and preferences. Freshly made pasta has a superior texture and flavor compared to store-bought pasta, making it the perfect foundation for a delicious and satisfying meal. Whether you are a seasoned cook or just starting out, making your own pasta is a fun and rewarding experience that is sure to impress your family and friends.

CHAPTER 1:
EQUIPMENT AND INGREDIENTS

1.1. Essential Equipment for Pasta Making

Making pasta at home requires some basic equipment, but you don't need to invest in a lot of fancy tools. Here is a list of essential equipment you'll need to get started:

1. Rolling Pin or Pasta Maker

A rolling pin or pasta maker is used to roll out the dough. If you don't have a pasta maker, a rolling pin will work just fine, but you will need to use more elbow grease! A rolling pin is a simple, traditional tool that is easy to use and can be found in many kitchens. A pasta machine, on the other hand, is a more specialized tool that can make the process of rolling out pasta faster and more efficient. It helps you roll out the dough evenly and creates the perfect thickness for your pasta. It works by feeding the dough through rollers that flatten and smooth it, and then through cutters that cut the dough into various pasta shapes. Pasta makers can be manual or electric and come in different sizes, styles, and price ranges. A pasta maker is a great investment for those who make pasta frequently, as it helps to achieve consistent results and saves time and effort compared to rolling and cutting the pasta by hand. When choosing a rolling pin or pasta machine, consider the thickness you would like to achieve and the level of control you need to make it happen.

2. Mixing Bowl

You will require a sizable mixing bowl to prepare the dough. The size of the mixing bowl should be large enough to accommodate the dough and allow for easy mixing and kneading. A stainless steel or glass bowl is a good option because it is sturdy, non-reactive, and easy to clean.

3. Cutting Board

A cutting board provides a flat and stable surface for rolling and cutting the pasta dough. It is also a useful surface for preparing ingredients, such as vegetables or cheese, to be added to the dough. A cutting board should be made of a material that is durable and non-reactive, such as bamboo, plastic, or maple. It is also important to have a cutting board that is large enough to accommodate the entire piece of pasta dough, as well as any other ingredients you may be using and is comfortable to work on.

4. Measuring Tools

Accurate measuring is key to making perfect pasta dough. Tools such as measuring cups, spoons, and a kitchen scale can help ensure hat the ingredients are correctly measured, and that the dough has the right texture and consistency. Measuring cups and spoons come in different sizes and materials and can be found at most kitchen supply stores. A kitchen scale can be especially useful for measuring ingredients like flour, which can vary greatly in volume depending on how it is packed.

5. Boiling Pot

A large pot with a lid is needed to boil the pasta. It should be deep enough to allow the pasta to cook freely and have enough water to prevent the pasta from sticking together. A pot that holds at least four to six quarts of water is ideal. A pot made of stainless steel or enameled cast iron is a good option as it is durable, easy to clean, and won't react with the pasta.

1.2. Common Ingredients Used in Pasta Making

1. Flour

Flour forms the base of pasta, and different types of flour have different properties that affect the texture, flavor, and color of the pasta. Durum wheat flour is the most common type of flour used in pasta making. It is commonly used to make pasta, as it is high in gluten, which helps the pasta to hold its shape and remain al dente even after cooking. Durum wheat flour is available in most grocery stores, either in its whole grain form or as semolina flour, which is finer and easier to work with.

2. Eggs

Eggs play a crucial role in pasta making as they provide both structure and flavor to the dough. Eggs are used in pasta recipes to provide richness and color, as well as to help the dough hold together. The number of eggs used in a recipe depends on the type of pasta being made, but typically one or two eggs are used per cup of flour. Fresh eggs are preferred for making pasta, as they have a more delicate flavor and a higher moisture content than store-bought eggs.

3. Salt

Salt helps to flavor the pasta and also serves as a preservative to help the dough last longer. It also helps to stabilize the gluten and improve the texture of the pasta. It should be added in moderation, as too much salt can make the pasta taste salty and unbalanced. A small pinch of salt is usually sufficient for most pasta recipes.

4. Water

Water is used in pasta recipes to help the dough come together and to adjust the consistency of the dough. The exact amount of H_2O [water] required depends solely on the type of pasta being made and the humidity in the kitchen, but typically one to two tablespoons of water are used per cup of flour.

5. Olive Oil

Olive oil is used in pasta recipes to add richness and flavor. It can also be used to help the dough come together, as well as to prevent the pasta from sticking together during cooking. A small amount of oil, such as one to two teaspoons, is typically added to the dough.

6. Other Ingredients

Some pasta recipes may call for additional ingredients to enhance flavor or color, such as spinach, beets, squid ink, or herbs. These ingredients should be added in small amounts and incorporated into the dough carefully to avoid overworking the dough or affecting its texture. If adding additional ingredients, it is important to rearrange the amount of fluid in the recipe accordingly to maintain the right consistency of the dough.

1.3. Substitutions and Variations for Ingredients

In this section, we will discuss different substitutions and variations that can be made to the common ingredients used in pasta making. These variations can cater to different dietary restrictions or preferences and add new dimensions of flavor to your pasta dishes.

1. Gluten-Free Pasta

For those with gluten sensitivities, gluten-free flour options such as almond flour, rice flour, or chickpea flour can be used instead of traditional wheat flour. These flours provide a suitable alternative for individuals with celiac disease, gluten intolerance, or those who simply choose to avoid gluten in their diet. It's crucial to note that, while these flours can be used in place of typical wheat pasta, they may have a slightly distinct flavor and texture.

When using gluten-free flour, it's recommended to find a blend specifically formulated for pasta making, as this will ensure that the dough holds together well and cooks evenly. Additionally, using xanthan gum or guar gum can help to enhance the elasticity and structure of the dough, making it easier to roll and cut.

It's important to remember that when making gluten-free pasta, the dough may be more delicate and prone to cracking. It may

also require longer resting times, so be patient and allow the dough to rest and hydrate before rolling and cutting. With a little effort and persistence, you'll be able to create delicious gluten-free pasta that's both satisfying and safe for those with gluten sensitivities.

2. Egg-Free Pasta

For those who are vegan or have an egg allergy, egg-free options such as aquafaba or flax seeds can be used instead of eggs in pasta dough. The liquid left over after draining a container of chickpeas, known as aquafaba, can be beaten into a cream to take the place of eggs in pasta dough. Eggs in pasta dough can be replaced with a gel-like substance made from flax seeds and water. These egg-free options provide a vegan alternative that is still able to hold the dough together and result in a delicious pasta dish.

3. Whole Grain

Using whole grain flour instead of all-purpose flour can add more nutrients and fiber to your pasta. Whole-grain flour is produced from the whole grain, including the bran, germ, and endosperm, whereas all-purpose flour is made from only the endosperm. This means that whole grain flour contains more fiber, vitamins, and minerals than all-purpose flour.

There are many different types of whole grain flour that can be used in pasta making, including whole wheat flour, spelt flour, and farro flour. Whole wheat flour is a popular choice and is made from hard red wheat. It has a nutty, slightly bitter flavor and a coarser texture than all-purpose flour. Another option is spelt flour, which is manufactured from an old grain that is more digestible than modern wheat. Farro flour is made from the Italian ancient grain emmer and has a slightly sweet, nutty flavor.

Using whole grain flour in pasta making will result in a denser, more toothsome pasta, but it can also be a bit more difficult to work with than all-purpose flour. You may need to add extra moisture or leave the dough to settle for an extended period of time. But the added nutrients and flavor make it well worth it!

4. Spices and Herbs

Spices and herbs can be added to pasta dough to enhance the flavor of the final product. A little bit goes a long way, so start with a small amount and adjust to taste. Herbs, such as basil, rosemary, or oregano, are traditional choices for pasta, while spices like chili flakes or black pepper can add a touch of heat. To add herbs, you can either finely chop them and mix them into the dough, or add them in a dried form, such as dried basil. For spices, a pinch or two will suffice. The flavor of the herbs and spices will infuse into the pasta as it cooks, providing a delicious aroma and taste.

5. Oils and Fats

Oils and fats play an important role in the texture of pasta dough. While traditional pasta recipes call for eggs as the source of moisture and richness, adding oils or fats can also provide these elements. Olive oil, avocado oil, coconut oil, and even butter, can all be used as an alternative to eggs, adding richness and depth to the flavor of the pasta. Consider using flavored oils, such as truffle oil or basil oil, to add a subtle but noticeable flavor to your pasta. It is recommended to use a light touch when adding oils and fats, as too much can make the pasta dough greasy and heavy. A general guideline is to add one to two tablespoons of oil or melted butter per cup of flour used in the dough recipe. This can be adjusted based on personal preference and the desired texture. Additionally, different types of liquids can be added to the pasta dough to create a different texture and taste. For example, adding wine, beer, or even coffee can add depth and complexity to the dough.

6. Cheeses

Adding cheese to pasta dough is a great way to elevate the flavor of your pasta. Different types of cheeses can add different flavor profiles to your pasta. For example, Parmesan cheese adds a nutty and salty flavor, Pecorino Romano cheese adds a tangy and salty flavor, and Gouda cheese adds a creamy and nutty flavor. When incorporating cheese into your pasta dough, it's important to use freshly grated cheese rather than pre-shredded cheese, as pre-shredded cheese often contains additives that can prevent it from melting smoothly. Additionally, you can adjust the amount of cheese you use to suit your desired flavor intensity.

7. Vegetables

Adding pureed or grated vegetables to pasta dough is a great way to add more nutrition and flavor to your pasta. The most common vegetables used in pasta dough include:

- Carrots: Adding pureed or grated carrots to your pasta dough will add a sweet and slightly earthy flavor, as well as a beautiful orange color.

- Sweet Potatoes: Sweet potato puree or grated sweet potatoes will add a natural sweetness and a beautiful orange color to your pasta dough.

- Zucchini: Adding grated zucchini to your pasta dough will add a subtle vegetable flavor and a green color. You can also add other types of squash to your pasta dough, such as butternut or acorn.

- Spinach: Adding pureed spinach to your pasta dough will add a bright green color and a mild leafy flavor to your pasta.

Note: When adding vegetables to your pasta dough, it is important to keep in mind that the additional moisture may affect the texture of the pasta. You may need to adjust the amount of flour or eggs used in your recipe to account for the extra moisture.

8. Other Variations

Adding other ingredients to your pasta dough can add flavor, texture, and color to your dishes. For example, incorporating spinach or beetroot puree into your dough can add a pop of green or red and also boost the nutritional content of your pasta. Another option is to use squid ink, which not only adds a bold and unique flavor but also turns the pasta an intriguing shade of black. There are endless possibilities when it pertains to ingredient variations, so feel free to get creative and experiment with different ingredients to find your favorite!

It is important to keep in mind that ingredient substitutions and variations may affect the texture and cooking time of your pasta, so it is recommended to start with a small batch and make adjustments as needed. The beauty of pasta making is that there is no right or wrong way, and you can customize your pasta to fit your unique preferences and tastes!

CHAPTER 2:
SHAPES AND FORMS OF PASTA

2.1. Overview of Different Pasta Shapes

Pasta shapes can also vary in size and thickness, which can affect the cooking time and texture of the pasta. For example, thinner pasta shapes like angel hair cook faster and are best suited for delicate sauces, while thicker shapes like pappardelle are best for hearty meat sauces.

In addition to the traditional shapes, there are also unique and unusual pasta shapes that can add interest to your pasta dishes, such as farfalle (bow tie), fusilli (spiral), and radiatori (radiator-like). These shapes can be a fun way to switch up your pasta game and bring new textures and flavors to your plate.

When choosing a pasta shape, it's also important to consider the sauce you will be serving with it. For example, a chunky tomato sauce will pair well with a shape that has ridges, such as penne or ziti, to help hold the sauce in place. A creamy sauce will work best with a smooth and wide shape, such as fettuccine or pappardelle.

Overall, the variety of pasta shapes available offers endless possibilities for creating delicious and unique pasta dishes in your own kitchen. There are three main categories: long pasta, short pasta, and stuffed pasta.

1. Long Pasta Shapes

Long pasta shapes are typically served with lighter sauces, as they are able to hold the sauce better than short pasta shapes. Examples of long pasta shapes include spaghetti, linguine, and fettuccine. These shapes are ideal for dishes such as spaghetti carbonara or pesto pasta.

Overall, long pasta shapes are a versatile option that can be utilised in many different kinds of pasta dishes. Whether you're serving a light and delicate tomato sauce or a rich and creamy Alfredo, long pasta shapes can be an excellent choice.

2. Short Pasta Shapes

Short pasta shapes are more versatile, as they can be served with light or heavier sauces. When cooking short pasta, it is important to keep an eye on the cooking time, as short pasta can overcook quickly. Al dente [to the tooth], or just firm enough to the bite, is the ideal texture for short pasta. Additionally, when serving short pasta with heavier sauces, it is vital to ensure that the pasta is well coated with sauce, as the smaller surface area of the pasta may not hold as much sauce as long pasta shapes. Examples of short pasta shapes include penne, macaroni, and rotini. These shapes are perfect for dishes like mac and cheese, or a hearty tomato sauce.

3. Stuffed Pasta Shapes

Stuffed pasta shapes offer a unique texture and flavor to pasta dishes. When it comes to stuffing pasta, the possibilities are endless. Some of the most popular fillings include cheese, such as ricotta or mozzarella, as well as meats such as ground beef, chicken, or pork. Vegetables such as spinach or mushrooms can also be used to create delicious and nutritious stuffed pasta shapes.

Additionally, the stuffing of the pasta can also affect the cooking time, as it will take longer for the pasta to cook through to the center. It is important to carefully monitor the cooking process and avoid over-cooking the pasta, as this can cause the filling to leak out or the pasta to become mushy.

When serving stuffed pasta, it is important to choose the right sauce to complement the flavors of the filling. A light tomato sauce, a creamy Alfredo sauce, or a flavorful broth can all be excellent options for enhancing the flavors of the stuffed pasta.
Examples of stuffed pasta shapes include ravioli, tortellini, and agnolotti.

In this book, we will be exploring all types of pasta shapes, giving you the tools to create a variety of delicious pasta dishes in your own kitchen.

2.2. Understanding the Purpose of Different Pasta Shapes

When it pertains to pasta preparations, one of the important things to consider is the shape. Different pasta shapes are designed for specific purposes and can greatly impact the overall taste and texture of your dish. Here are three important factors to remember when selecting a pasta shape:

1. Shape and Sauce Pairings

Different pasta shapes are meant to be paired with different sauces. Thicker sauces tend to cling better to thicker pasta shapes, while lighter sauces work best with thin, delicate pasta shapes. For example, thin spaghetti works well with light sauces, while fettuccine is best paired with rich, creamy sauces. Additionally, some sauces, such as a hearty tomato sauce, can overpower delicate pasta shapes, so it is best to choose a shape that can hold its own against the sauce. Understanding the right pairing can make all the difference in the overall taste of your dish.

2. Shape and Cooking Time

The shape of pasta can also impact the cooking time. Thinner pasta shapes will cook faster, while thicker shapes will take longer to cook. Thinner pasta shapes like spaghetti and angel hair can cook in as little as two to three minutes, while thicker shapes like fettuccine or pappardelle can take upwards of ten minutes or more to cook properly. It's important to keep this in mind when planning your meal and timing the different components of your dish.

3. Shape and Texture

Lastly, the shape of pasta can also impact the texture. Thicker shapes tend to hold their shape better, while thinner shapes can break down more easily. Understanding the texture of each pasta shape can help you choose the right one for your dish and ensure a perfect end result.

2.3. Techniques for Making Different Pasta Shapes

In this section, we'll dive into the techniques for making different pasta shapes. We'll cover rolling techniques using both a pasta maker and a rolling pin, cutting techniques for long and short pasta shapes, and techniques for making stuffed pasta like ravioli, tortellini, and agnolotti. This section will give you a comprehensive understanding of the different techniques for making a variety of pasta shapes, ensuring that you're able to create pasta with the desired shape and texture.

1. Rolling Techniques

Rolling Techniques are a crucial part of making different pasta shapes. The thickness of the dough directly affects the texture and cooking time of the final product. Here are some of the most popular rolling techniques:

- Hand-Rolling: This is the traditional method of rolling out pasta dough. It requires a lot of practice and patience, but yields excellent results. To hand-roll pasta, you'll need a rolling pin and a flat surface. Start by dividing the dough into small portions and flatten each one into a disc. Roll the disc out, rotating it and flipping it as you go, until it reaches your desired thickness.

- Rolling with a Pasta Maker: If you have a pasta maker, rolling pasta is made even easier. Simply attach the pasta maker to the rolling attachment and pass the dough through the machine, adjusting the rollers to the desired thickness. The pasta maker will also cut the pasta into your desired shape, making the process even more effortless.

2. Cutting Techniques

Cutting techniques are an essential aspect of pasta making as they determine the final shape and texture of the pasta. There are three common cutting techniques used in pasta making: knife cutting, pasta machine cutting, and sheeter cutting.

- Knife Cutting: This is the traditional method of cutting pasta and can be done using a large, sharp kitchen knife. The dough is completely rolled out into a unique thin sheet and then cut into desired shapes using the knife. This method is best for simple shapes, such as fettuccine, linguine, and pappardelle.

- Pasta Machine Cutting: This method uses a pasta machine to cut the dough into desired shapes. The dough is fed through the machine, and a particular cutting attachment is used to create the desired shape. This method is best for creating uniform and consistent pasta shapes.

- Sheeter Cutting: A sheeter is a large machine that is used to roll and cut the dough into thin sheets. This method is best for making delicate and thin pasta shapes such as lasagna and wonton wrappers. The dough is fed through the sheeter, which flattens and cuts it into sheets of a desired thickness.

3. Stuffed Pasta Techniques

Stuffed pasta shapes are a delicious way to enjoy a pasta dish with a hearty filling. The techniques for forming stuffed pasta shapes can vary depending on the shape, the filling, and personal preference. Below are a few of the most used techniques for forming stuffed pasta:

- Hand-Forming: This technique involves hand-shaping the pasta dough around the filling. The dough is usually rolled into a thin sheet, the filling is placed in small spoonfuls at regular intervals, and then the edges of the dough are pinched together to form the shape. This

technique requires a delicate touch and good hand control, but the resulting shapes are often irregular and unique.

- Pasta Machine Forming: Some pasta machines come with a special attachment that allows you to form stuffed pasta shapes. The dough is passed through the machine, and the filling is added as it comes out. The machine then folds the dough over the filling and seals it to form the shape. This method is fast and efficient but can result in uniform shapes that lack character.

- Mould-Forming: Mould-forming involves using a special shaped mould to form the pasta. The dough is completely rolled into a unique thin sheet and then pressed into the mould. The filling is added, and then the mould is removed to reveal the shape. This method is often used for intricate shapes and results in consistent, well-defined shapes.

- Cutter-Forming: Cutter-forming involves using a special cutter to form the pasta. The dough is completely rolled into a unique thin sheet and then cut into rounds or squares. The filling is added to the center, and then the edges are pinched together to form the shape. This method is often used for simple shapes and results in quick, easy-to-make stuffed pasta shapes.

2.4. Popular Shapes of Pasta

1. Spaghetti

This is one of the most recognizable pasta shapes in the world. It is a long, thin noodle that is perfect for tossing with sauces or for use in soups and stews. The round, cylindrical shape of spaghetti makes it ideal for capturing sauces and flavors, making it one of the most versatile pasta shapes available. Spaghetti is made from semolina flour and water and is typically cut into long strands that are about 1/8 inch thick. When cooked, it has a tender, firm texture that is perfect for holding onto sauces, which makes it a popular choice for many Italian dishes, including classic pasta with marinara sauce or spaghetti carbonara. Whether served with a simple tomato sauce or a more elaborate dish, spaghetti is sure to be a hit with pasta lovers everywhere.

Here are the step-by-step instructions to make spaghetti pasta by hand:

Ingredients:
- 2 cups of semolina flour
- 2 cups of all-purpose flour
- 4 eggs
- 1/2 teaspoon of salt
- Water

Equipment:
- Large mixing bowl
- Fork or whisk
- Wooden board
- Rolling pin
- Knife
- Pasta drying rack or towel

Instructions:

1. In a large mixing bowl, combine the semolina flour, all-purpose flour, and salt. Mix the dry ingredients together.
2. Create a small well in the middle of the flour mixture and add the eggs. Utilising a whisk or fork, stir the eggs and start to incorporate the flour gradually until a dough starts to form.
3. Knead the dough on a moderately floured surface for approximately ten minutes until it becomes smooth and elastic. Add a little water to the dough if it's too dry to moisten it. If it's too wet, add more flour.
4. After kneading the dough, cover it completely with a moist towel or plastic wrap and allow it to rest for at least thirty minutes.
5. Divide the whole dough into four equal portions and take one piece of dough. Flatten it very well with a pasta machine or a dowel [rolling pin] until it becomes thin enough to pass through the thinnest setting of the machine.
6. Dust the dough with flour and roll it through the spaghetti cutter on the machine. If you don't have a pasta machine, use a dowel [rolling pin] to level the dough, then cut it into thin strips with a knife.
7. Hang the spaghetti on a pasta drying rack or place it on a clean towel to dry for a few hours.
8. Once the spaghetti is dry, boil a pot of salted water and cook the pasta for two to three minutes or until it's al dente.
9. Drain the spaghetti and serve with your favorite sauce and toppings.
10. Enjoy your handmade spaghetti!

2. Fettuccine

This is a type of pasta that is long, flat, and ribbon-like in shape. This pasta shape is typically made with eggs and is often paired with sauces that are thick and creamy, such as Alfredo sauce. The wide, flat shape of fettuccine allows the sauce to easily coat each strand, resulting in a delicious and flavorful bite. This pasta is also well suited for dishes with chunky meat and vegetable sauces, as the flat shape provides ample surface area for the ingredients to cling to. Fettuccine is a staple in many Italian-style dishes and is a popular choice for many home cooks and restaurant chefs alike. It can be produced from a number of different ingredients, including wheat flour, semolina, or other grains, and can be paired with an array of flavorful sauces, herbs, and spices to create a satisfying and delicious meal.

Here are detailed directions for making fettuccine pasta by hand:

Ingredients:
- 2 cups all-purpose flour
- 2 large eggs
- 1/2 teaspoons salt
- Water

Equipment:
- Mixing bowl
- Rolling pin or pasta machine
- Knife

Instructions:

1. Add the salt and flour to a mixing dish and make a well in the center.
2. Crack the selected eggs into the hole and stir them with a fork.
3. Slowly begin to incorporate the flour into the cracked eggs with the fork. Once it becomes too difficult to use the fork, switch to using your hands.
4. Knead the dough for about ten to fifteen minutes or until it becomes smooth and elastic. Add just a little H2O [water] to the dough if it's too dry to moisten it; if it's too wet, add more flour.
5. Form the dough into a ball and wrap it in plastic wrap. Leave it to settle at room temperature for about thirty minutes.
6. The dough should be rolled out to a depth of about 1/8 inch using a rolling pin or pasta machine on a clean surface dusted with flour.
7. If using a rolling pin, fold the dough in half and roll it out again. Repeat this entire process a few more times until the dough becomes very thin.
8. Once the dough is thin enough, use a knife or pasta cutter to cut the dough into strips that are about 1/4 inch wide for fettuccine.
9. Dust the fettuccine noodles with flour to prevent them from sticking together.
10. Bring a sizable saucepan of salted water to the point of boiling, then add the fettuccine. Cook for about two to four minutes or until the pasta is al dente.
11. Drain the yummy looking pasta and serve with your preferred sauce and toppings.

3. Linguine

This is a popular shape of pasta that is narrow and flat, similar to fettuccine but thinner. It originated from Italy and is a staple in Italian dishes. The acronym "linguine" gets its name from the Italian term "lingua" meaning "tongue" which is a reference to its long, flat shape that resembles a tongue. Linguine is typically made from semolina flour, eggs, and water, but variations may include additional ingredients such as spinach or squid ink for added flavor and color. It is a multifaceted pasta that can smoothly be paired with a variety of sauces, including light and creamy sauces like pesto, olive oil and lemon, or heavier sauces like tomato-based sauces or clam sauce. Linguine is also popular in dishes that incorporate seafood, such as clam linguine or shrimp linguine, where the long shape of the pasta helps to hold on to the ingredients and flavor. Additionally, linguine can be served cold in salads or as a main course in pasta dishes. Overall, linguine is a delicious and versatile pasta that is popular in Italian cuisine and beyond, making it a great addition to any pasta repertoire.

Here are the step-by-step instructions to make linguine pasta by hand:

Ingredients:
- 2 cups of all-purpose flour
- 2 large eggs
- 1/2 teaspoon salt
- Water

Equipment:
- Large mixing bowl
- Fork or whisk
- Clean surface or board for kneading and rolling out the dough
- Rolling pin
- Sharp knife
- Linguine attachment for pasta maker (optional)

Instructions:

1. Start by mixing the flour and salt in a large mixing bowl.
2. In a different dish, mix the selected eggs together.
3. Create a unique hole in the middle of the flour mixture and pour the beaten eggs into it.
4. Using a fork or whisk, begin to mix the eggs and flour together, starting from the center and working your way out.
5. Once the mixture begins to come together and form a nice dough, proceed by using your hands to knead the dough for about ten minutes, until it is smooth and elastic.
6. Let the dough settle for at least thirty minutes after covering it with a cleaned kitchen cloth.
7. Once the dough has rested, dust a clean surface or board with flour and begin to gently spread the dough out on to the surface to get your preferred thickness.
8. Cut the dough into thin strips about 1/8 to 1/4 inch wide.
9. To make the linguine shape, either use a sharp knife to hand-cut the strips into long, thin noodles, or use a linguine attachment for your pasta maker.
10. If hand-cutting the noodles, lightly dust them with flour to prevent sticking.
11. To cook the linguine, bring a sizable saucepan of salted H2O [water] to the point of boiling, then add noodles. Prepare for three to five minutes, or till firm [al dente].
12. Drain the noodles, and toss with your favorite sauce and toppings.
13. Serve immediately and enjoy your handmade linguine pasta!

4. Lasagna

This is a flat, wide pasta noodle that is often used in layered dishes. The name "lasagna" comes from the Greek word "lasagnum," meaning "chamber pot," due to its wide and flat shape that resembles a shallow dish. The traditional Italian lasagna is made with flat sheets of pasta, layered with cheese, meat, tomato sauce, and seasonings, then baked in the oven until the cheese is melted and bubbly. The versatility of lasagna pasta makes it a popular choice for a wide variety of dishes, ranging from classic lasagna, to lasagna roll-ups, to vegetarian lasagna. The flat shape of the pasta allows it to hold on to sauces and ingredients well, making it an excellent choice for hearty, satisfying dishes.

Here are the step-by-step instructions on how to make lasagna pasta by hand:

Ingredients:
- 2 cups all-purpose flour
- 2 large eggs
- 1/4 teaspoon salt
- Water (if needed)

Equipment:
- Large mixing bowl
- Fork
- Rolling pin
- Large knife or pasta cutter

Instructions:

1. Start by making the pasta dough. In a sizable mixing dish, stir together the salt and all-purpose flour. Make a hole in the middle of the flour mixture.
2. Crack the eggs into the well and use a fork to beat them together. Start to gradually mix in the flour from the sides of the well into the eggs.
3. When the dough begins to form together, knead it with your hands for at least eight to ten minutes, or till it is soft and elastic. In case the dough is extremely dry, pour in a few droplets of water to help it come together.
4. After kneading the dough, seal it with aluminium foil and set it aside for thirty minutes.
5. After thirty minutes, dust your work surface moderately with flour and utilise a dowel [rolling pin] to roll out the pasta dough to a thin sheet. Keep dusting the surface with flour to prevent sticking.
6. Cut the rolled-out pasta dough into long, rectangular strips that are about four inches wide and eight inches long. These will be the lasagna sheets.
7. Bring a large pot of salted water to a boil. Add the lasagna sheets to the boiling water and cook for one to two minutes until they are just tender. Be careful not to overcook the pasta.
8. Retrieve the cooked lasagna sheets from the hot boiling water with a slotted spoon [any design] and drop them in a big bowl of cold water to halt the cooking process. Once cooled, lay the lasagna sheets out on a clean surface to dry.
9. You can now use the lasagna sheets to make your lasagna dish by layering them with your chosen sauce and filling ingredients.
10. Enjoy your homemade lasagna pasta!

5. Tortellini

This is a small, ring-shaped pasta that is often filled with cheese, meat, or a combination of the two. It originated in the Emilia-Romagna region of Italy and is a staple in traditional Italian cuisine. Tortellini can be served in soup or tossed with a sauce, and it is often paired with rich, flavorful sauces such as a creamy Alfredo or a hearty meat ragù. The small size of the pasta makes it perfect for snacking or for serving as a main course. Additionally, its unique shape makes it a visually appealing addition to any dish, and it is sure to impress guests at a dinner party.

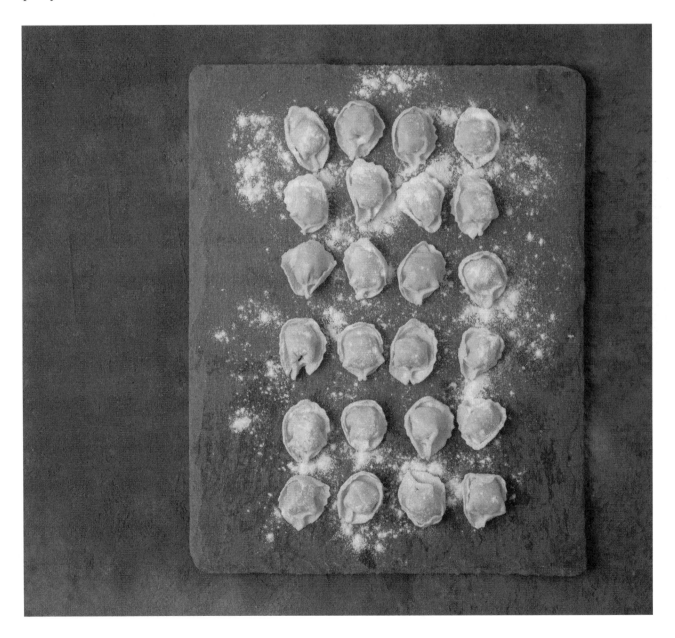

Here are the step-by-step instructions on how to make tortellini pasta by hand:

Ingredients:
- 2 cups all-purpose flour
- 2 large eggs
- 1/2 teaspoon salt
- 1/4 cup water

Equipment:
- Rolling pin
- Pastry cutter or sharp knife
- Small bowl of water
- Towel

Instructions:

1. In a sizable mixing dish, put together salt and flour. Make a well in the center and crack in the eggs. Beat the eggs with a fork until they are well mixed.
2. Gradually start incorporating the flour from the edges into the egg mixture with a fork until a dough forms.
3. Knead the dough with your hands for at least eight to ten minutes or until it is soft and elastic. in case the dough is extremely dry, pour in a few droplets of water; if it is too sticky, increase the amount of flour.
4. Make a ball out of the dough and swaddle it in a towel. Let it rest for thirty minutes at room temperature.
5. Cut off a small piece of the dough, roughly the size of a walnut, and roll it out into a thin sheet with a rolling pin. Dust the surface with flour if the dough is sticking.
6. Use a pastry cutter or a sharp knife to cut the sheet into two-inch squares.
7. Place a small dollop of filling (such as cheese, meat or vegetables) in the center of each square.
8. Dip your finger in the small bowl of water and run it around the edge of the square to moisten it.
9. Fold the square in half diagonally to make a triangle, pressing the edges together to seal the filling inside.
10. Take the two corners of the triangle farthest from the fold and bring them together, pressing them firmly to seal. The tortellini should now resemble a small hat or naval shape.
11. Repeat the entire process with the leftover dough and filling.
12. Boil the tortellini in salted water for at least two to three minutes or till they float to the top.
13. Drain the tortellini and serve with your favorite sauce or broth. Enjoy!

6. Gnocchi

This is a type of pasta that originates from Italy. It is made from a mixture of potatoes and flour, and sometimes also includes eggs. The dough is formed into small, pillow-like shapes and is traditionally served with a tomato-based sauce or a butter and sage sauce. Gnocchi can also be baked, sauteed, or fried, making it a versatile and popular pasta dish. The texture of gnocchi is soft and light, making it a favorite among children and adults alike. Because of its simple and classic taste, gnocchi is a staple in many Italian households and is enjoyed by pasta lovers all over the world.

Here are the step-by-step instructions on how to make gnocchi pasta by hand:

Ingredients:
- 2 pounds of potatoes
- 1 and 1/2 cups of all-purpose flour
- 1 egg
- 1 teaspoon of salt

Equipment:
- Large pot for boiling the potatoes
- Potato ricer or masher
- Large flat surface
- Clean kitchen towel
- Knife
- Fork

Instructions:

1. Begin by bringing the potatoes to a boiling point in a sizable saucepan until they are soft and fully cooked. This should take around twenty to twenty-five minutes.
2. When the potatoes are ready, drain the water from the potatoes and set them aside to settle for just a few minutes. When they're cold enough to touch, peel the potato's skin and throw it away.
3. Mash the potatoes with a potato masher or ricer until completely smooth as well as lump-free.
4. On a large flat surface, create a well with the mashed potatoes and add the flour, salt, and egg in the center.
5. Using a fork, mix the flour, egg, and salt into the mashed potatoes. Mix it well until the dough becomes smooth and consistent.
6. Hand-knead the dough for a few minutes, or until it turns firm and elastic. You can add more flour if the dough is too sticky.
7. Split the dough into tiny chunks and roll each one into a long, slim rope approximately one inch thick.
8. Use a knife to cut the rope into small bite-sized pieces, about one inch long.
9. To create the characteristic grooves on each gnocchi, use a fork to press and roll each piece of dough against the tines of the fork.
10. Once you have created the desired number of gnocchi pieces, place them onto a clean kitchen towel to dry.
11. To cook the gnocchi, bring a large pot of salted water to a boil. Add your desired quantity of the gnocchi to the boiling water [H2O] and cook for about two to three minutes, or until they rise to the very top of the boiling water.
12. Once the gnocchi is cooked, drain them and serve them with your favorite sauce or toppings. Enjoy!

7. Pappardelle

This is a type of pasta that is characterized by its wide, flat, and ribbon-like shape. It is similar in appearance to fettuccine, but it is wider and a bit more substantial in texture. This type of pasta is ideal for hearty sauces and ragù, as the wide surface area allows for maximum sauce adherence. Pappardelle is typically made with a mixture of all-purpose flour, eggs, and salt, and it can be purchased fresh or dried. Some variations of pappardelle include additions of spinach or other herbs to add flavor and color to the pasta. Whether served with a classic tomato sauce, a creamy mushroom sauce, or a rich meat sauce, pappardelle is a versatile and delicious pasta that is perfect for any meal.

Here are the step-by-step instructions to make pappardelle pasta by hand:

Ingredients:
- 2 cups all-purpose flour
- 2 large eggs
- 1/2 teaspoon salt
- 1-2 tablespoons of water (as needed)

Equipment:
- Rolling pin
- Large pot
- Colander
- Clean surface to work on

Instructions:

1. In a large mixing bowl, combine the all-purpose flour and salt. Make a well in the center of the mixture.
2. Crack the eggs into the hole and utilise a fork to stir them all together, gradually incorporating the flour as you whisk.
3. Immediately, when the dough begins to come together, continue using your bare hands to knead it until it is smooth and elastic, about ten minutes. If the dough is too dry, add one to two tablespoons of water as needed.
4. Cover the dough inplastic wrap and let it settle at room temperature for at least thirty minutes.
5. On a moderately floured surface, utilise a dowel [rolling pin] to spread out the dough to about 1/8 inch thickness.
6. Use a sharp knife or a pasta cutter to cut the pasta into long, wide strips about one inch wide.
7. Dust the pasta strips with flour to prevent sticking, then roll them into loose nests and let them dry on a floured surface for ten to fifteen minutes.
8. Bring a large pot of salted water to a boil. Add the pappardelle strips to the pot and stir gently to prevent sticking.
9. Cook the pappardelle for about three to five minutes, or until al dente.
10. Once ready for consumption, use a colander to drain the yummy pasta and serve immediately with your favorite sauce and toppings.
11. Enjoy your homemade pappardelle pasta!

8. Tagliatelle

This is a type of flat pasta that is similar in shape to fettuccine but slightly narrower. It is traditionally made with egg and flour and is typically used in dishes such as Bolognese, carbonara, and mushroom sauces. This type of pasta is also a popular choice for making pasta salads and casseroles. The long, thin strands of tagliatelle allow it to easily soak up and hold onto sauces, making it a delicious option for many pasta dishes. Similar to pappardelle, these noodles are often used in dishes like tagliatelle alla carbonara.

Here are the step-by-step instructions to make tagliatelle pasta by hand:

Ingredients:
- 2 cups all-purpose flour
- 2 large eggs
- 3-4 tablespoons water
- Pinch of salt

Equipment:
- Large mixing bowl
- Fork
- Rolling pin
- Knife
- Flour sifter
- Large pot
- Colander

Instructions:
1. Make a unique well in the middle of the flour after sifting it into a sizable mixing dish.
2. Crack the eggs into the well and add a pinch of salt.
3. Utilise a fork to whisk the eggs and gradually mix in the flour until the dough forms a rough mass.
4. Knead the dough with your bear-hands until it becomes smooth and elastic, about five to seven minutes.
5. If the dough is too dry, add a teaspoon of water [H2O] at a time till the dough reaches the desired consistency.
6. Seal the made dough with a wet cloth and allow it to settle for about thirty minutes.
7. Divide the dough into smaller portions for easier handling.
8. Dust a clean work surface with flour.
9. Take one portion of the dough and flatten it into a disk with a rolling pin.
10. Starting from the thickest setting on your pasta machine, pass the dough through the rollers several times, gradually decreasing the thickness until you reach your desired thickness.
11. If you don't have a pasta machine, use the dowel [rolling pin] to spread the dough to about 1/8 inch in thickness.
12. Cut out the sheet of pasta into twelve-inch lengths.
13. Dust the pasta sheets with flour and then fold them over a few times to create several layers.
14. Use a sharp knife to cut the folded sheets into strips of your desired width, usually about 1/4 inch for tagliatelle.
15. Unfold the strips and dust them with flour to prevent sticking.
16. Bring a large pot of salted water to a boil.
17. Add the tagliatelle strips to the boiling water and cook for about two to three minutes or until al dente.
18. Utilising a colander, drain the yummy pasta and serve with your favorite sauce.

9. Udon

This is a type of thick, chewy noodle popular in Japanese cuisine. It is manufactured from grain flour and water respectively, and is typically served in soups, stir-fries, or hot pot dishes. Udon noodles have a neutral flavor and a soft, smooth texture, making them versatile enough to pair with a wide range of sauces and ingredients. They are often garnished with green onions, nori (dried seaweed), and other flavorful toppings, and are considered a staple in Japanese cooking.

Below are step-by-step procedures on how to prepare udon pasta by hand:

Ingredients:
- 2 cups of all-purpose flour
- 1/2 teaspoon of salt
- 3/4 cup of warm water

Equipment:
- Mixing bowl
- Rolling pin
- Udon knife or sharp knife

Instructions:

1. In a mixing bowl, mix the flour and salt together.
2. Slowly pour in the warm water and stir with a fork or your hand until the dough comes together.
3. Knead the dough with your hand for at least ten minutes until it turns soft and elastic.
4. Seal the dough with a plastic wrap and allow it to settle for thirty minutes.
5. After the dough has rested, dust the surface moderately with flour and spread the dough out to about 1/4 inch thickness.
6. Using the udon knife or sharp knife, cut the dough into thin strips, about 1/4 inch wide.
7. Dust the strips with flour to prevent them from sticking together.
8. Hold each strip of dough by the ends and stretch it gently with your hands, shaking off any excess flour.
9. Place the stretched dough on a floured surface and repeat with the remaining dough strips.
10. Once all the dough strips have been stretched, place a sizable saucepan of water on the cooker to boil.
11. Add the udon pasta to the boiling water and cook for eight to ten minutes or until it reaches your desired texture.
12. Drain the udon pasta and rinse with cold water to stop the cooking process.
13. Serve the udon pasta with your favorite sauce or broth. Enjoy!

10. Soba

This is another Asian-style noodle. Soba is thin and made from buckwheat flour, making it a popular option for gluten-free diets. It carries a nutty, earth-like flavor that merges well with light broths, sauces, and other ingredients. Soba can be served hot or cold, and is often enjoyed in soup dishes, stir-fries, or served chilled with dipping sauces. Soba is a versatile and nutritious pasta option, and is especially popular in the summertime for its refreshing and light quality.

Below are step-by-step procedures on how to prepare soba pasta by hand:

Ingredients:
- 2 cups of soba flour (buckwheat flour)
- 1/2 cup of all-purpose flour
- 3/4 cup of water
- Additional flour for dusting

Equipment:
- Mixing bowl
- Rolling pin
- Knife
- Clean cloth or drying rack

Instructions:

1. Combine soba flour and all-purpose flour in a mixing bowl.
2. Add water gradually to the flour mixture while stirring with a fork. Mix the dough until it forms a ball.
3. Dust a clean surface with additional flour.
4. Stand the dough on the dusted floured surface and begin kneading it for about five to ten minutes until it becomes smooth and elastic.
5. Once the dough is smooth, flatten it out with a dowel [rolling pin] into a lengthy, thin sheet.
6. Cut the sheet of dough into rectangular strips of about seven to ten centimeters in length and two centimeters in width.
7. Dust the strips with flour and stack them on top of each other.
8. Cut the stacked strips into thin slices, about two millimeters in width.
9. Use your hands to separate the sliced dough strands and lightly dust them with flour to prevent them from sticking together.
10. Bring a pot of salted water to a boil.
11. Add the soba strands to the boiling water and stir them gently to prevent them from sticking together.
12. Boil the soba strands for about five to seven minutes, or until they are cooked to your desired consistency.
13. Once the soba strands are cooked, using a colander, drain and rinse them underneath cold running H20 [water] to remove excess starch.

11. Farfalle

Also known as bowtie pasta, is a popular shape of pasta that is made up of small, flat pieces that are pinched in the middle to create a butterfly or bowtie shape. This versatile pasta can be merged with different types of sauces and spices, making it a popular choice for both light and hearty pasta dishes. Farfalle is often used in salads, soups, and casseroles, as well as in classic pasta dishes such as Carbonara and Primavera. The unique shape of farfalle also makes it a fun and playful ingredient for creative and artistic presentations.

Here are the step-by-step instructions to make farfalle pasta by hand:

Ingredients:
- 2 cups of all-purpose flour
- 3 eggs
- 1 tablespoon of olive oil
- 1/2 teaspoon of salt
- Water

Equipment:
- Mixing bowl
- Fork
- Rolling pin
- Knife
- Farfalle pasta cutter (optional)

Instructions:

1. Put in the salt and flour to a sizable bowl and make a well in the center.
2. Crack the eggs into the well and add the olive oil.
3. Using a fork, whisk the eggs and slowly start incorporating the flour from the edges.
4. Keep mixing until the dough starts to come together, and it's too difficult to mix with the fork.
5. knead the dough using your bare hands for at least five to ten minutes until it's smooth and elastic.
6. Make a ball shape with the dough, seal it with plastic wrap, and allow it to settle for thirty minutes.
7. After the dough has rested, flour your working surface and spread the dough out into a thin sheet with a rolling pin.
8. Cut the sheet into long strips about 1 1/2 inches wide and then cut each strip into rectangles about one inch wide.
9. Take each rectangle and fold it in half, pressing down on the top edge to create a crease in the middle of the rectangle.
10. Pinch the sides of the rectangle together to form a bowtie shape.
11. Repeat the process with the remaining rectangles until all the pasta has been formed into the farfalle shape.
12. If you have a farfalle pasta cutter, you can use it to trim the edges of the bowties to make them more uniform.
13. Once all the pasta is formed, bring a sizable saucepan of water that is salted to a boiling point and cook the farfalle for two to three minutes until it's al dente.
14. Drain the pasta and serve with your favorite sauce or toppings. Enjoy!

12. Penne

Penne is a cylindrical shaped pasta that is cut diagonally at both ends into short, tube-like pieces. The name "penne" is derived from the Italian term for "pen," which points to the design of the pasta. Penne is a versatile pasta that can be paired with a variety of sauces, from light and creamy to rich and meaty. Its shape and texture make it an excellent choice for pasta salads and baked pasta dishes. Whether it's served with a classic tomato sauce, a creamy Alfredo sauce, or a spicy arrabbiata sauce, penne is always a crowd-pleaser.

Here are the step-by-step instructions on how to make penne pasta by hand:

Ingredients:
- 2 cups of all-purpose flour
- 2 large eggs
- 1 tablespoon of water
- Semolina flour for dusting

Equipment:
- Mixing bowl
- Fork
- Rolling pin
- Knife
- Penne pasta mold (optional)

Instructions:
1. Sift the all-purpose flour into a mixing bowl to remove any lumps.
2. Make a unique well in the middle of the selected flour and crack the eggs into it.
3. Use a fork to beat the eggs, then gradually mix in the flour until it forms a rough dough.
4. Knead the ball of dough for at least ten minutes on a floured board, or until it is smooth and elastic.
5. Let the ball of dough to settle for at least thirty minutes, covered with a moist cloth.
6. Divide the dough into smaller portions, dust with semolina flour, and roll each portion into a thin sheet with a rolling pin.
7. Cut the rolled-out dough into small rectangles about 1 inch by 1 1/2 inch.
8. Take each rectangle and roll it around a penne pasta mold or a wooden skewer, pressing firmly so that the dough wraps tightly around the mold.
9. Slide the penne pasta off the mold and let it dry on a floured surface for about thirty minutes.
10. Bring a saucepan of water that is salted to a boiling point and add the penne pasta. Cook for six to eight minutes or until the pasta is al dente.
11. Drain the water and serve the penne pasta with your favorite sauce and toppings.
12. Enjoy your homemade Penne pasta!

13. Ravioli

Ravioli is a filled pasta that is made by placing a filling, such as cheese or meat, between two thin layers of pasta dough. The edges of the pasta dough are then sealed to enclose the filling. Ravioli is often served in a broth or with a sauce and is a popular dish in Italian cuisine. It is also available in different types of shapes as well as sizes, from square to round, and can be infused with different types of spices to suit different tastes and preferences.

Here are the step-by-step instructions on how to make ravioli pasta by hand:

Ingredients:
- 2 cups all-purpose flour
- 3 large eggs
- 1/2 teaspoon salt
- 1 tablespoon olive oil

Equipment:
- Large mixing bowl
- Fork
- Rolling pin
- Ravioli cutter or knife

Instructions:

1. In a sizable mixing dish, put together the flour and salt. Create a well in the middle of the flour mixture.
2. Crack the eggs into the well and add the olive oil.
3. Using a fork, beat the eggs and olive oil, gradually incorporating the flour from the sides of the well.
4. Once the mixture begins to combine together, utilise your bare hands to knead the ball of dough until it becomes smooth and elastic. This should take about five to ten minutes.
5. Once the dough is ready, wrap it in plastic wrap and allow the dough to settle for approximately thirty minutes.
6. When the dough has settled, shear it into four portions.
7. Take one portion of the dough and roll it out into a thin sheet using a rolling pin. The sheet should be thin but not so thin that it tears easily.
8. Once the sheet is the desired thickness, use a ravioli cutter or knife to cut the sheet into individual squares.
9. Place a small spoonful of filling in the center of each square.
10. Brush the edges of the square with a little bit of water to help the pasta stick together.
11. Fold the square in half to create a triangle shape, pressing the edges together to seal.
12. Use the tines of a fork to press down on the edges of the ravioli to ensure they are well-sealed.
13. Repeat the process with the remaining sheets of dough and filling.
14. Once all the ravioli are assembled, bring a large pot of salted water to a boil.
15. Gently place the ravioli in the boiling water and cook for two to three minutes or until they float to the surface.
16. Use a slotted spoon to remove the ravioli from the water and serve with your favorite sauce.

14. Orecchiette

Orecchiette - meaning "little ears" in Italian, is a type of pasta that is commonly found in Southern Italy. The pasta is shaped like small, circular disks with a dimple in the center and a slightly raised rim. Orecchiette is traditionally made with semolina flour and water, although other flours can also be used. It is usually paired with thick, hearty sauces such as ragù or chunky vegetable sauces, as the ridges of the pasta help to hold on to the sauce. Orecchiette is also sometimes used in soup dishes, where the pasta acts as a scoop to hold onto ingredients such as beans or vegetables. Overall, orecchiette is a versatile pasta shape that adds texture and depth to any dish.

Here are the step-by-step instructions for making orecchiette pasta by hand:

Ingredients:
- 2 cups of all-purpose flour
- 2 eggs
- 1/4 teaspoon of salt
- 1/4 cup of water

Equipment:
- Mixing bowl
- Fork
- Cutting board
- Knife
- Measuring cups
- Rolling pin

Instructions:
1. Combine the flour and salt in a mixing dish and make a well in the middle.
2. Put in the eggs and water into the hole and utilise a fork to stir them all together.
3. Gradually mix in the flour from the edges of the well until a dough forms.
4. Knead the ball of dough on a moderately floured surface for at least ten minutes until it turns soft and elastic.
5. Divide the dough into small pieces and roll each piece into a rope about 1/2 inch in diameter.
6. Cut the ropes into small pieces that are about 1/2 inch long.
7. Take each small piece of dough and use a knife to flatten it into an oval shape.
8. Use your right or left thumb to hold down firmly on the center of the oval and push it forward, while using your other hand to roll the dough slightly backwards.
9. Place the shaped pasta on a floured cutting board and repeat the process until all the dough has been used.
10. Allow the pasta to dry off for at least thirty minutes before cooking it in boiling salted water for approximately eight to ten minutes max or until it is firm [al dente].
11. Serve the pasta with your favorite sauce and toppings.

15. Capellini (Angel Hair)

Capellini pasta, also known as angel hair, is a thin and delicate pasta shape that is perfect for light sauces and broths. This pasta is characterized by its thin, long, and cylindrical shape that resembles hair. It is best served with simple sauces like garlic and olive oil or with broths, soups, and salads. Due to its delicate nature, angel hair pasta should be cooked quickly in boiling water, usually for two to three minutes, to avoid overcooking and breaking.

Here are the step-by-step instructions for making capellini pasta by hand:

Ingredients:
- 2 cups of all-purpose flour
- 2 large eggs
- 1/2 teaspoon salt
- Water, as needed

Equipment:
- Rolling pin
- Knife or pasta cutter
- Clean surface for kneading

Instructions:
1. Sift the flour onto a clean surface and create a well in the center.
2. Crack the eggs into the center of the well and add the salt.
3. Using a fork, gradually start mixing the flour with the eggs until the dough starts to form.
4. Utilise your bare hands to knead the ball of dough till it becomes smooth and elastic.
5. If the ball of dough is extremely dry, add H2O [water], one teaspoon at a time as you see fit, till it becomes moist enough to knead.
6. Once the dough is ready, cover it with plastic wrap and let it rest for thirty minutes.
7. Unwrap the dough and cut it into four equal pieces.
8. Roll one piece of dough into a thin sheet using a rolling pin.
9. Dust the sheet with flour and fold it several times until it forms a compact rectangle.
10. Use a sharp knife or a pasta cutter to slice the rectangle into thin strips.
11. Unfold the strips and let them dry for about five to ten minutes.
12. Repeat this process with the remaining pieces of dough until all the pasta is cut into capellini.
13. Cook the capellini in a pot of salted boiling water for about two to three minutes, or until it's al dente.
14. With a colander drain the pasta and serve it with your best sauce and toppings.

16. Fusilli (spiral)

Fusilli is a twisted pasta shape that is often used in cold pasta salads, baked pasta dishes, or with sauces that can cling to the twists. This shape is also commonly used for pasta sculptures, as the twists hold the sauce well. Fusilli is a versatile shape that can be paired with a variety of sauces, from light and fresh tomato sauces to rich and creamy Alfredo sauces.

Here are the step-by-step instructions to make fusilli pasta shape by hand:

Ingredients:
- 2 cups of all-purpose flour
- 3 eggs
- 1 tablespoon of olive oil
- 1/2 teaspoon of salt
- Water, as needed

Equipment:
- Mixing bowl
- Fork or whisk
- Pasta machine or rolling pin
- Wooden skewer or chopstick

Instructions:

1. In a sizable mixing dish, put together the salt and the flour.
2. Create a unique well in the middle of the flour mixture and add in the eggs and olive oil.
3. Utilise a whisk or fork to stir the eggs and slowly incorporate the flour until a dough comes to life.
4. Knead the ball of dough on a lightly floured surface for approximately five to seven minutes until it turns soft and elastic.
5. Seal it with a moist cloth and allow it to rest for thirty minutes.
6. When the ball of dough has settled, slice it into small pieces and roll each piece out into long, thin ropes about 1/4 inch in diameter.
7. Cut the ropes into small pieces about 1 inch long.
8. Take each piece and roll it on a floured surface using your fingers to form a thin rope.
9. Take a wooden skewer or chopstick and wrap the pasta rope around it, pressing down gently with your fingers as you roll it.
10. Once the pasta is wrapped around the skewer or chopstick, slide it off and let it dry for a few minutes.
11. Continue with the rest of the dough until you have made enough Fusilli pasta.
12. Cook the fusilli pasta in boiling water for eight to ten minutes until al dente.
13. Serve with your favorite sauce and toppings.
14. Enjoy your homemade fusilli pasta!

17. Radiatori (radiator-like)

Radiatori is a short, curved pasta shape that resembles small radiators. This shape is ideal for dishes that have chunkier sauces, as the curves and ridges hold on to the sauce well. Radiatori is also commonly used in pasta salads, as the shape holds up well to cold pasta dishes. This pasta shape is also great for baked pasta dishes, as it can hold a lot of sauce and cheese in the curves.

Below are step-by-step guidelines on how to prepare radiatori pasta by hand:

Ingredients:
- 2 cups of all-purpose flour
- 2 eggs
- 1/2 teaspoons salt
- 1/4 cup water

Equipment:
- mixing bowl
- fork
- rolling pin
- knife
- radiatori pasta board (optional)

Instructions:

1. In a sizable mixing dish, put together the salt and flour. Make a unique well in the middle of the flour mixture.
2. Crack the eggs into the well and use a fork to whisk the eggs, gradually incorporating the flour until a rough dough forms.
3. Add water [H20], a tablespoon at a time as you see fit, and continue mixing until the dough comes together into a smooth and elastic ball. Knead the dough for five to seven minutes.
4. Flatten the dough into a disc and wrap with plastic wrap. Let the dough settle for at least thirty minutes.
5. On a moderately floured surface, spread the dough out into a thin sheet. You can utilise a dowel [rolling pin] or a pasta machine to achieve this.
6. Using a knife, cut the dough into small rectangles that are roughly 1 inch long and 1/2 inch wide.
7. To shape the radiatori, hold one of the rectangles lengthwise and use your fingers to pinch and fold one of the long edges inwards, creating a twist. Repeat this process with the other long edge.
8. Press the twisted ends together to create a short, curled cylinder.
9. Place the radiatori on a floured surface or a radiatori pasta board to dry for at least thirty minutes.
10. Once the pasta has dried, you can cook it in salted boiling water for two to three minutes, or until al dente. Serve with your favorite sauce or toppings.

18. Agnolotti

Agnolotti is a type of stuffed pasta shape that gets its origin from the Piedmon District of Italy. The name "agnolotti" means "little lambs" in Italian, and this pasta shape is traditionally shaped like small, plump pillows. Agnolotti is typically filled with ingredients such as cheese, meat, or vegetables, and is often served with a light sauce or broth that allows the flavors of the filling to shine through. This pasta shape is considered a type of "filled pasta" and is a popular dish in Italian cuisine.

Here are the step-by-step instructions to make Agnolotti pasta shape by hand:

Ingredients:
- 2 cups of all-purpose flour
- 2 eggs
- 1/2 teaspoon of salt
- Water (as needed)

Equipment:
- Mixing bowl
- Fork
- Rolling pin
- Knife or pasta cutter
- Flat surface (floured)

Instructions:

1. In a mixing bowl, combine the all-purpose flour and salt. Make a well in the middle of the flour mixture.
2. Crack the selected eggs into the hole and stir them with a fork, gradually mixing in the flour from the sides of the well.
3. Once the dough comes together, knead it with your hands until it's smooth and elastic. Add a few drops of water if the dough is too dry or a bit of flour if it's too sticky.
4. Cover the dough with a cloth and let it rest for about thirty minutes.
5. After the dough has rested, lightly flour a surface and spread the dough out with a rolling pin until it's about 1/8 inch thick.
6. Using a pasta cutter or knife, slice the flatten dough into small squares that are roughly two inches wide.
7. To form each agnolotti, place a small spoonful of filling in the center of each square.
8. Fold one corner of the square over the filling to form a triangle, pressing the edges together to seal the filling inside.
9. Using your fingers, fold the two opposite corners of the triangle together, pressing them together to form a hat-like shape.
10. Repeat the process until you've used up all the dough and filling.
11. Cook the agnolotti in a pot of boiling, salted water for two to three minutes or until they float to the surface.
12. Drain the agnolotti and serve with your favorite sauce.
13. Enjoy your homemade agnolotti pasta!

19. Rotini

Rotini is a unique kind of pasta that is curly or corkscrew shaped. It is commonly used in pasta salads and casseroles, as well as in dishes like pesto and marinara. The ridges and curves of rotini make it a good choice for holding sauces and ingredients, making it a flexible option for hundreds of different recipes. It can be produced with a combination of different flours and ingredients, including semolina, whole wheat, and even spinach or tomato-based pastas. Because of its shape, rotini is also popular for its ability to be paired with a variety of different ingredients and sauces, from heavy, creamy sauces to light and simple vinaigrettes.

Here are the step-by-step instructions on how to make rotini pasta by hand:

Ingredients:
- 2 cups of all-purpose flour
- 2 large eggs
- 1/4 cup of water
- 1 teaspoon of salt

Equipment:
- Mixing bowl
- Fork
- Rolling pin
- Knife
- Rotini pasta maker (optional)

Instructions:
1. In a sizable mixing dish, put together the salt and flour, then make a well in the center.
2. Beat the eggs in a separate bowl, then pour them into the well.
3. Use a fork to mix the flour and eggs together, adding water a little at a time to help combine the ingredients into a dough.
4. Work the dough on a lightly floured surface until it becomes smooth and elastic, about ten minutes.
5. Shear the dough into four pieces and roll each one into a ball.
6. Take one of the dough balls and flatten it with a rolling pin until it is about 1/8 inch thick.
7. Use any cutter to slice the dough into strips that are about 1/2 inch wide.
8. Take each strip and twist it into a spiral shape, creating the characteristic helix shape of rotini pasta.
9. Cut the twisted pasta into short lengths, about one inch long.
10. Repeat with the rest of the dough balls until all the pasta is made.
11. Prepare the rotini pasta in a saucepan of boiling water that has been salted for eight to ten minutes or until al dente.
12. Drain the pasta and serve with your favorite sauce and toppings.

If you have a rotini pasta maker, you can use it to create the spiral shape more easily. Simply feed the strips of pasta through the rotini maker and it will do the twisting for you.

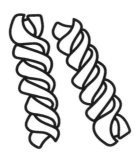

20. Conchiglie (shells)

Conchiglie are a popular type of pasta that are known for their distinctive shape, which resembles a small, scalloped seashell. They are often used in soups, salads, and baked dishes, as they are able to hold on to sauces and ingredients well. Conchiglie are versatile and can be paired with a variety of flavors and ingredients, from bold, spicy tomato sauces to creamy, cheese-based sauces. They are also popular for their ability to retain their texture and shape, even after cooking, making them an ideal pasta for a variety of dishes. Whether you are making a quick weeknight dinner or preparing a more elaborate meal, conchiglie are a staple pasta that should definitely be included in your pantry.

Here are the step-by-step instructions to make conchiglie pasta by hand:

Ingredients:
- 2 cups of all-purpose flour
- 3 large eggs
- 1 tablespoon of olive oil
- 1 teaspoon of salt
- Water

Equipment:
- Large mixing bowl
- Wooden cutting board
- Rolling pin
- Knife
- Conchiglie pasta mold (optional)

Instructions:
1. In a large mixing bowl, combine the all-purpose flour and salt, and make a well in the center of the mixture.
2. Crack the eggs into the well and add the olive oil.
3. Using your fingers or fork, gently whisk the flour into the eggs until the mixture forms a rough dough.
4. Work the dough on a lightly floured surface for at least five to ten minutes, or until it becomes smooth and elastic.
5. Cover the dough with a clean cloth and allow it to settle for approximately thirty minutes.
6. When the dough has settled, slice it into small pieces that are easy to handle.
7. Roll each piece into a thin sheet, about 1/8 inch thick.
8. Using a knife or a pastry cutter, cut the sheet into small squares, about one inch by one inch.
9. With your right or left thumb along with your index finger, softly pinch one corner of a square and roll the pasta square around your finger.
10. Pinch the other corner of the square and press it against the rolled pasta to create a shell shape.
11. Repeat the process for the remaining squares.
12. Let the conchiglie dry for about thirty minutes before cooking them in a pot of salted boiling water for at least eight to ten minutes maximum, or until firm [al dente].

If you have a conchiglie pasta mold, you can also use it to shape the pasta. Simply place the square pasta sheet over the mold and press it gently to create the shell shape.

In summary, there are many popular shapes of pasta that are commonly used in a variety of dishes. While many of these shapes may seem similar, they each have unique characteristics that make them perfect for different types of sauces and preparations.

As for the differences between spaghetti and linguine, the most significant difference is their thickness. Spaghetti is thinner than linguine and therefore cooks more quickly. Fettuccine, papadelle, and tagliatelle are all long, flat shapes of pasta, but they differ in their widths and thicknesses. Fettuccine is the widest and thickest, while tagliatelle is the thinnest and most delicate.

When it comes to stuffed pasta, ravioli and agnolotti are similar, but agnolotti are typically smaller and more rounded, while ravioli are larger and square-shaped. The fillings for these two pastas can also vary significantly.

Finally, rotini and fusilli are both spiral-shaped pastas, but rotini has a tighter spiral, while fusilli has a looser, corkscrew-shaped spiral. This subtle difference can affect the way the pasta holds sauces and other ingredients, making each shape ideal for different types of dishes.

Understanding the differences between these pasta shapes can help you choose the right one for your next dish and enhance your overall pasta experience.

CHAPTER 3:
MAKING THE PERFECT PASTA DOUGH

3.1. Understanding Gluten Development in Pasta Dough

Gluten is a unique protein that is present in wheat as well as other grains that gives pasta dough its elasticity and strength. In order for pasta dough to have the perfect texture and hold its shape during cooking, it's extremely important to comprehend the role of gluten development in the dough-making process.

Gluten is formed when the proteins in the flour are hydrated and mixed, causing the proteins to bond together. The more the dough is kneaded, the stronger the gluten network becomes. Over-kneading the dough, however, can result in a tough, rubbery texture.

To achieve the optimal gluten development in pasta dough, it is important to mix the dough until it comes together and then knead it for a moderate amount of time, usually around five to seven minutes. The dough should be smooth and not too sticky, but still pliable.

It is also necessary to let enough time for the dough to settle after kneading, as this allows the gluten to relax and makes it easier to roll out the dough into desired shapes.

In summary, understanding the role of gluten development in pasta dough is key to creating the perfect texture and flavor in your pasta dishes. With a little effort and persistence, you will be capable of mastering the art of gluten development in no time!

3.2. Basic Pasta Dough Recipe

Making your own pasta is a fulfilling and delicious experience, allowing you to control the flavor and texture of your pasta. This basic pasta dough recipe is a great starting point, but feel free to add your own personal touch by experimenting with different ingredients and techniques.

1. Measurement and Ingredients
The following is a basic recipe for pasta dough which yields approximately four servings:

Ingredients:
- 2 cups of all-purpose flour
- 3 large eggs
- 1 teaspoon of salt
- 1 tablespoon of olive oil (optional)

2. Directions for Mixing
1. In a sizeable mixing dish, stir together the flour and salt.
2. Crack the eggs into a well in the center of the flour mixture.
3. Use a fork to beat the eggs and gradually add the flour first from the well's sides until a rough dough forms.
4. Drizzle the olive oil over the dough and continue to mix until the dough comes together in a ball.

3. Kneading and Resting

Spread the piece of dough onto a moderately floured surface and begin kneading for at least five to ten minutes until smooth and elastic.

Form a ball out of the dough and set it in a dish. Let the dough settle in the dish for thirty minutes to one hour, covered with aluminium foil.

Note: The resting time permits the gluten [protein] in the beautiful dough to settle, which makes it simpler to roll as well as shape. After resting, the dough can be stored in the refrigerator for up to two days.

3.3. Variations of Pasta Dough

While the basic pasta dough recipe is a staple in every pasta-making kitchen, there are also several variations that can be made to add more flavor, nutrition, or accommodate dietary restrictions. Here are six common variations of pasta dough:

1. Whole Grain Pasta Dough

To make a whole grain pasta, simply replace some or all of the all-purpose flour with a whole grain flour of your choice, such as whole wheat, spelt, or quinoa flour. Keep in mind that whole grain flour will change the texture of the pasta and may require slightly more liquid than traditional pasta dough.

Ingredients:
- 2 cups whole wheat flour
- 2 cups all-purpose flour
- 4 large eggs
- 1 teaspoon salt
- 2 tablespoons olive oil

Instructions:
1. In a sizable dish, stir together the whole wheat flour and all-purpose flour.
2. Create a well in the center of the flour
3. mixture and add in the eggs, salt, and olive oil.
4. Use a fork to beat the eggs and slowly incorporate the flour from the sides of the well into the eggs.
5. Once the mixture becomes too difficult to stir with a fork, use your hands to continue kneading the dough till it is super smooth and feels elastic.
6. Divide the dough into four equal parts and shape each part into a ball.
7. Cover the balls of dough with a damp cloth and let them rest for at least thirty minutes.
8. After the dough has rested, utilise a rolling pin [a dowel] to flatten each unique ball into a thin sheet.
9. Cut the pasta into the desired shape.
10. Allow the pasta to air dry for at least one hour before cooking.
11. Boil the pasta in a large pot of salted water for two to three minutes, or until al dente.
12. Enjoy your delicious whole grain pasta!

2. Semolina Pasta Dough

Made from semolina flour, this type of pasta dough is coarser and denser than egg-based pasta dough. This dough is ideal for making rustic, hearty pasta dishes. It is often used for making traditional Italian pasta shapes, such as spaghetti and penne, as it holds its shape well and has a slightly chewy texture.

Ingredients:

- 2 cups semolina flour
- 2 large eggs
- 1/4 teaspoon salt
- 2 tablespoons water (or more if needed)

Instructions:

1. In a sizable mixing dish, stir together the semolina flour and salt.
2. Make a sizable hole in the middle of the flour mixture and crack in the eggs.
3. Using a fork, beat the eggs and gradually mix in the flour until a crumbly mixture forms.
4. Add two tablespoons of water to the mixture and beat till the dough forms together. If the dough seems dry, add more water, one tablespoon at a time, until it is smooth and not too sticky.
5. Pour the dough onto a lightly floured surface and work on it for approximately ten minutes or until it is smooth and elastic.
6. Wrap the dough in plastic wrap and let it rest for about thirty minutes.
7. Roll out the dough using a rolling pin or pasta machine to your desired thickness.
8. Cut the dough into your desired shape and cook the pasta in boiling salted water for two to three minutes.
9. Serve with your favorite sauce or toppings.
10. Enjoy your homemade semolina pasta!

3. Gluten-Free Pasta Dough

For those who are gluten intolerant, there are several gluten-free flours that can be used to make pasta dough. Popular options include rice flour, corn flour, and chickpea flour. You can also find pre-made gluten-free pasta flour blends in stores.

Ingredients:
- 2 cups gluten-free all-purpose flour
- 2 large eggs
- 1 teaspoon salt
- 1-2 tablespoons olive oil

Instructions:
1. In a large mixing bowl, combine the gluten-free flour, eggs, salt, and one tablespoon of olive oil.
2. Mix until the ingredients form a rough dough. In case the dough is extremely dry, add an additional tablespoon of olive oil.
3. Pour the dough onto a moderately floured surface and knead for about five minutes or until smooth and elastic.
4. Cover the entire dough with plastic wrap and let it rest for thirty minutes.
5. After resting, roll out the dough to your preferred thickness and slice into your preferred shape.
6. Boil the pasta in a large pot of salted water until it is cooked to your liking, usually two to three minutes.
7. Drain the pasta and serve with your favorite sauce.

Note: You can add additional flavors to the pasta dough such as garlic, herbs, or spices to make it more interesting.

4. Egg-Free Pasta Dough

Making egg-free pasta is simple. Just leave out the eggs in the basic pasta dough recipe and increase the amount of water slightly.

Ingredients:
- 2 1/2 cups all-purpose flour
- 1/2 teaspoon salt
- 1/2 teaspoon olive oil
- 3/4 cup warm water

Instructions:

1. In a sizable mixing dish, stir together the salt and flour.
2. Make a sizable hole in the middle of the mixture and add in the olive oil and warm water.
3. Using a fork, mix the ingredients together until the dough starts to come together.
4. Pour out the dough onto a lightly floured surface and knead for about five minutes, or until smooth and elastic.
5. Seal the entire dough with plastic wrap and allow it to settle for approximately thirty minutes.
6. After resting, cut the dough into pieces and roll it out into your desired shape.
7. Cook the pasta in boiling salted water for two to three minutes, or until it is al dente.
8. Serve with your favorite sauce and enjoy!

5. Herbed Pasta Dough

Adding herbs to pasta dough can give it a delicious, fragrant flavor. Try adding dried or fresh basil, oregano, or rosemary to your pasta dough.

Ingredients:

- 2 cups all-purpose flour
- 3 large eggs
- 2 teaspoons dried basil
- 1 teaspoon dried oregano
- 1 teaspoon dried thyme
- 1 teaspoon dried rosemary
- Salt to taste

Instructions:

1. In a sizable dish, stir together the thyme, flour, eggs, dried basil, oregano, rosemary, and salt until the dough starts to come together.
2. Work the entire dough on a moderately floured surface until it forms a smooth, elastic ball, about ten minutes.
3. Wrap the dough in plastic wrap and let it rest for thirty minutes to an hour.
4. Divide the dough into several pieces and roll out into thin sheets, either by hand or with a pasta machine.
5. Cut the sheets into the desired shape of pasta.
6. Allow the pasta to dry for a few minutes before cooking.
7. Boil the pasta in salted water for two to three minutes or until al dente, then drain and serve with your favorite sauce.
8. Enjoy your homemade herbed pasta, filled with the fragrant flavors of basil, oregano, thyme, and rosemary!

6. Spiced Pasta Dough

Adding spices such as turmeric, paprika, or red pepper flakes can add a pop of flavor and color to your pasta dough. Experiment with different spice combinations to find the perfect match for your taste buds.

Ingredients:
- 2 cups of all-purpose flour
- 3 large eggs
- 1 teaspoon of ground black pepper
- 1 teaspoon of dried basil
- 1 teaspoon of dried oregano
- 1 teaspoon of dried thyme
- 1 teaspoon of dried rosemary
- 1 teaspoon of garlic powder
- 1 teaspoon of red pepper flakes (optional)
- 1 teaspoon of salt

Instructions:
1. In a sizable mixing bowl, stir together the all-purpose flour, eggs, black pepper, basil, oregano, thyme, rosemary, garlic powder, red pepper flakes (if using), and salt until a rough dough forms.
2. On a clean, floured surface, knead the dough for about ten minutes, until smooth and elastic.
3. Cover the entire dough with plastic wrap and allow it to settle for approximately thirty minutes to allow the flavors to develop.
4. Divide the dough into four to six portions, roll each portion into a thin sheet using a rolling pin, and cut into the desired pasta shape.
5. Cook the pasta in a pot of boiling salted
6. water for two to four minutes, or until al dente.
7. Serve the pasta with your favorite sauce and toppings.

Note: This recipe yields enough dough to serve four to six people. If you are making pasta for a larger group, simply double or triple the recipe.

7. Spinach pasta dough

Spinach pasta dough is a variation of traditional pasta dough that uses spinach puree in place of some or all of the water used to make the dough. The addition of spinach not only adds a pop of color to the pasta, but also provides a boost of nutrients, including vitamins A and C, iron, and calcium.

Ingredients:

- 2 cups all-purpose flour
- 2 cups spinach puree (blanched and drained)
- 4 large eggs

Instructions:

1. In a sizable mixing bowl, put together the spinach puree and flour. Make a well in the middle of the flour blend and add the eggs.
2. Use a fork to beat the eggs and gradually incorporate the flour mixture until a soft dough forms.
3. Pour out the dough onto a lightly floured surface and knead it until it becomes completely soft and elastic. This should take a maximum of ten minutes.
4. Cover the entire dough in plastic wrap and let it rest for thirty minutes to allow the gluten to develop.
5. Roll the dough out using a pasta machine or rolling pin, and cut it into your desired shape.
6. The bright green color and tender texture of spinach pasta dough makes it a beautiful addition to any dish, and the added nutrients make it a healthier option than traditional pasta dough.

8. Beetroot pasta

Beetroot pasta is a colorful and nutritious alternative to traditional wheat pasta. This variation of pasta dough is made by combining cooked, pureed beetroot with flour and eggs to create a bright red dough.

Beetroot pasta is a fun and flavorful addition to any pasta dish. Its natural sweetness pairs well with earthy flavors such as mushrooms and spinach, as well as bold and spicy sauces.

Ingredients:

- 1 large beetroot, peeled and boiled
- 2 cups of all-purpose flour
- 2 large eggs
- 1 tablespoon of olive oil

Instructions:

1. Begin by boiling the beetroot until it is tender, then remove from heat and let cool.
2. Once cooled, puree the beetroot in a food processor until smooth.
3. In a sizable mixing dish, put together the pureed beetroot, flour, eggs, and olive oil.
4. Mix until the ingredients form a dough.
5. Work the dough on a lightly floured surface for at least five minutes, until it turns soft and elastic.
6. Wrap the dough in plastic wrap and let it rest for thirty minutes.
7. Roll out the dough using a pasta machine or a rolling pin, and cut into desired shapes.
8. Serve your homemade beetroot pasta as a main meal or as an accompaniment dish with a simple tomato sauce or a creamy goat cheese sauce. Enjoy!

9. Carrot Pasta Dough

Carrot Pasta Dough is a fun and colorful variation of traditional pasta dough that is made by incorporating grated carrots into the dough. The carrots add a natural sweetness and a vibrant orange hue to the pasta. This pasta dough is ideal for making fettuccine or pappardelle, and it pairs well with a variety of sauces, from creamy to tomato-based.

Ingredients:
- 2 cups of all-purpose flour
- 3 large eggs
- 1 cup of grated carrots
- 1 teaspoon of salt

Instructions:
1. In a sizable dish, whisk together the grated carrots, flour, eggs, and salt until a dough forms.
2. Work the entire dough on a moderately floured surface for approximately ten minutes, until it turns super smooth as well as elastic.
3. Wrap the dough in plastic wrap and let it rest for thirty minutes.
4. Roll out the dough and cut it into desired shapes or use a pasta machine to hape it.
5. Cook the pasta in a pot of boiling salted water for two to three minutes or until al dente.
6. Carrot Pasta Dough is a tasty and nutritious twist on traditional pasta that is ideal for adding a splash of color to your dish. Try serving it with a simple tomato sauce, or pair it with a creamy Alfredo sauce for a delicious and satisfying meal.

10. Sun-Dried Tomato Pasta Dough

Sun-dried tomato pasta dough is a variation of traditional pasta dough that incorporates sun-dried tomatoes for added flavor and color. This type of pasta dough is perfect for those who love bold, intense flavors and a pop of color on their plate and it can be used in a variety of pasta dishes, from simple tomato sauces to hearty meat sauces.

Ingredients:
- 1 cup of all-purpose flour
- 1/4 cup of finely chopped sun-dried tomatoes
- 2 large eggs
- Salt to taste
- Water (if needed)

Instructions:
1. In a sizable dish, put together the sun-dried tomatoes, flour, eggs, and salt.
2. Use a fork to mix the ingredients together until they form a crumbly mixture.
3. Gradually add water, a little at a time, until the mixture forms a soft and pliable dough.
4. Knead the entire dough on a lightly floured surface for about five to seven minutes, until smooth and elastic.
5. Cover the entire dough in plastic wrap and allow it to settle for about thirty minutes.
6. Roll the dough out using a rolling pin or pasta machine, then cut it into desired shapes.
7. Cook the pasta in boiling salted water for two to three minutes or until al dente.
8. Serve with your favorite sauce and enjoy!

Each type of pasta dough has its own unique properties and benefits, and it is important to choose the right type of dough for the desired result. Whether you prefer a chewy texture, a rich, buttery flavor, or a gluten-free option, there is a pasta dough for every taste and occasion.

3.4. Tips for Successful Pasta Making

1. Importance of Temperature and Humidity

Pasta making is a delicate process and a number of factors contribute to the success of your final product. Humidity and temperature are both extremely important. For the dough to come together and form the right consistency, it is crucial to have the right temperature. Warmer and more humid conditions can lead to stickier and softer dough, while drier and cooler conditions can result in a drier and harder dough. Pasta dough is best made in a cool, dry environment. To ensure success, try to make pasta on a day with low humidity and a room temperature around 68-72°F. Additionally, be sure to store the flour and eggs at room temperature for at least an hour before making the dough.

2. Measuring Accuracy

Measuring accuracy is essential in pasta making, as even small deviations in ingredients can significantly affect the final outcome of the pasta. The recommended measurement for flour is to use a kitchen scale to ensure the exact amount required for the recipe. For liquids, such as eggs and water, it's best to use a measuring cup. Additionally, it's important to follow the recipe's instructions precisely, as different recipes may call for different ratios of ingredients. Over-kneading the dough or adding too much liquid can result in tough, dense pasta. On the other hand, not kneading the dough enough or adding too little liquid can result in crumbly, dry pasta. By following the recipe and measuring ingredients accurately, you can achieve the perfect texture and flavor for your homemade pasta.

3. Proper Kneading and Resting

Proper kneading and resting are critical steps in making successful pasta dough. Kneading properly helps to build the gluten [protein] in the dough, which gives it structure and strength. The amount of time you have to knead the dough will vary depending on the type of dough you are making and the recipe you are using. However, an overall rule of thumb is to knead for about eight to ten minutes, or until the dough is smooth and elastic. After kneading, it's important to allow the dough to rest for a period of time. This allows the gluten to relax and makes it easier to roll out the dough. The rest time will vary depending on the recipe, but a common range is thirty minutes to two hours. During this time, you can cover the dough with moist cloth or plastic wrap to prevent it from drying out. After resting, your dough should be easy to roll out and cut into the desired shape. If the dough is still too firm or difficult to work with, give it a little more time to rest. If it is too soft or sticky, you may need to add more flour or refrigerate it for a short time to firm it up. Avoiding over-handling: Over-handling the dough can make it tough and difficult to work with. So, handle the dough gently and avoid over-kneading or over-rolling. If the dough becomes too difficult to work with, cover it and let it rest for a few minutes.

4. Other Tips and Tricks

Experiment with different ingredients and techniques to create unique pasta dishes. Consider adding spices, herbs, or vegetables to the pasta dough for added flavour. Preserve leftover pasta in an airtight container and use it within a few days.

Here are some other tips and tricks to help you achieve success in pasta making:

- Dust the surface and rolling pin [dowel] with flour to prevent sticking.
- Use a generous amount of flour when rolling out the dough to prevent sticking.
- Use a very sharp knife or cutter to ensure clean cuts. A pasta machine can save you time and effort by evenly rolling out the dough and cutting it into the desired shape.
- If the pasta dough is too dry, add a small amount of water and mix it in. In case the dough is extremely sticky, add a small amount of flour and mix it in.
- Use high-quality ingredients: Fresh and high-quality ingredients ensure that your pasta has a consistent texture and taste. Using good-quality flour, eggs, and seasonings will enhance the flavor of your pasta.
- Keep your work surface clean and dry: Ensure that your work surface is dry and free of any oil or moisture to prevent your dough from sticking.
- Store the pasta properly: After cutting the pasta, it is vital to preserve the dough properly in order for it not to dry out. You can either hang it on a pasta drying rack or dust it with semolina flour and store it in an airtight container.
- Practice makes perfect: Making pasta is an art that takes time and practice to perfect. Don't feel disappointed if your very first try in making pasta doesn't turn out perfectly. Keep trying and experimenting with different recipes and ingredients to find the perfect pasta for you.

CHAPTER 4:
PASTA RECIPES

4.1. SPAGHETTI

1. Classic Spaghetti

Ingredients:
- 1 pound spaghetti
- 4 quarts water
- 2 teaspoons salt
- 2 tablespoons olive oil

Instructions:
1. Fill a sizable saucepan with four quarts of H2O [water] and bring it to a rolling boil.
2. Add two teaspoons of salt and two tablespoons of olive oil to the boiling water.
3. Carefully add the spaghetti to the pot and cook for approximately eight to ten minutes max or until it becomes firm [al dente].
4. Drain the spaghetti and serve with your desired sauce or toppings.
5. Enjoy your homemade spaghetti!

2. Spaghetti with Pesto Sauce

Ingredients:
- 1 pound spaghetti
- 1 cup fresh basil leaves
- 1/2 cup freshly grated Parmesan cheese
- 1/2 cup pine nuts
- 3 cloves of garlic, minced
- 1/2 cup extra-virgin olive oil
- Salt and pepper to taste

Instructions:
1. Cook spaghetti for eight to ten minutes or until al dente. Drain and set aside.
2. In a food processing machine, add the pine nuts, basil leaves, Parmesan cheese, and minced garlic. Pulse until coarsely chopped.
3. Slowly add the extra-virgin olive oil while the food processor is running, until the mixture becomes a smooth paste.
4. Sprinkle the pesto with pepper and salt to taste.
5. Shake and toss the cooked spaghetti with the pesto sauce and serve immediately, garnished with extra Parmesan cheese if desired.

3. Spaghetti with Meatballs

Ingredients:

- 1 pound spaghetti
- 1 pound ground beef or ground pork
- 1/2 cup breadcrumbs
- 1/2 cup grated Parmesan cheese
- 2 cloves of garlic, minced
- 2 eggs
- Salt and pepper to taste
- 2 tablespoons olive oil
- 2 tablespoons butter
- 1 can (14.5 ounces) diced tomatoes
- Fresh parsley for garnish

Instructions:

1. In a sizable dish, stir together the Parmesan cheese, eggs, ground beef or pork, breadcrumbs, garlic, salt, and pepper.
2. Roll the mixture into 1 1/2-inch meatballs.
3. Heat up the olive oil as well as the butter in a sizable dish over moderate heat.
4. Add the meatballs to the pan and cook till completely browned on both sides, for at leastfive minutes.
5. Throw in the diced tomatoes to the pan and bring the sauce to a simmer.
6. Let the sauce cook until it thickens slightly, about ten minutes.
7. Meanwhile, fill up a sizable pot with four quarts of H2O [water] and ensure it comes to a rolling boil.
8. Add two tablespoons of salt to the boiling water.
9. Add one pound of spaghetti to the pot and stir occasionally to prevent clumping.
10. Cook spaghetti for eight to ten minutes or until al dente.
11. Drain the spaghetti and divide it among four plates.
12. Spoon the meatball sauce over the spaghetti and garnish with fresh parsley. Serve hot.

4.1. SPAGHETTI

4. Spaghetti Carbonara

Ingredients:
- 1 pound spaghetti
- 4 large eggs
- 1/2 cup grated Pecorino Romano cheese
- 1/2 cup grated Parmesan cheese
- 1/2 teaspoon black pepper
- 4 ounces pancetta or bacon, diced
- 2 cloves garlic, minced

Instructions:
1. Prepare spaghetti in a sizable saucepan of salted boiling water until al dente, about eight to ten minutes.
2. In a different bowl, stir together the black pepper, eggs, Pecorino Romano cheese, and Parmesan cheese.
3. In a large skillet, cook the pancetta or bacon over medium heat until crispy.
4. Add the chopped-up garlic onto the skillet and prepare for another one minute.
5. Strain the spaghetti and combine it with to the skillet, with the pancetta, and garlic. Toss to blend all together.
6. Take-off the skillet from the cooker and bring in the egg and cheese mixture to the pasta, tossing quickly to prevent the eggs from scrambling.
7. Serve immediately with additional grated cheese and black pepper. Enjoy!

5. Spaghetti Aglio e Olio

Ingredients:
- 1 pound spaghetti
- 6 cloves garlic, minced
- 1/2 cup extra-virgin olive oil
- Salt and black pepper to taste
- 1/4 cup chopped parsley
- 1/4 cup grated Parmesan cheese (optional)

Instructions:
1. Fill a sizable pot with four quarts of H2O [water] and bring to a rolling boil.
2. Add two tablespoons of salt to the boiling water.
3. Add one pound of spaghetti to the pot and stir occasionally to prevent clumping.
4. Cook spaghetti for eight to ten minutes or until al dente. Reserve one cup of pasta water.

5. Drain spaghetti and set aside.

6. In a large saucepan, heat the olive oil over moderate heat. Put the chopped garlic in the pan and prepare until lightly golden and fragrant, about two to three minutes.

7. Add the prepared spaghetti to the saucepan and stir to combine with the garlic and olive oil.

8. Add 1/2 cup of pasta water and salt and pepper to taste. Stir until the spaghetti is coated in the sauce.

9. Stir in chopped parsley and grated Parmesan cheese, if desired. Serve hot.

4.2. FETTUCCINE

1. Fettuccine with Chicken and Broccoli

Ingredients:

- 1 pound fettuccine pasta
- 1 pound boneless chicken breasts, cut into 1-inch pieces
- 2 tablespoons olive oil
- 1 broccoli head, chopped into tiny florets

- 2 cloves of garlic, minced
- 2 cups heavy cream
- Salt and pepper to taste
- 1 cup grated Parmesan cheese
- Fresh parsley for garnish

Instructions:

1. Fill a sizable pot with four quarts of H20 [water] and bring to a rolling boil.
2. Add two tablespoons of salt to the boiling water.
3. Add one pound of fettuccine to the pot and stir occasionally to prevent clumping.
4. Prepare the fettuccine until it becomes firm or al dente, which means it should be tender but still firm to the bite. Fresh fettuccine typically takes about two to three minutes to cook, while dried fettuccine may take up to eight minutes.
5. In a sizable skillet, warm the olive oil over moderatetemperature.
6. Put the chicken in the pan and cook until golden brown, about five to seven minutes.
7. Put the broccoli into the pot and prepare until tender, about three to four minutes.
8. Add the chopped garlic to the pot and cook until fragrant, about three seconds.
9. Add the heavy cream and boil.
10. Reduce the heat to low and let it simmer for two to three minutes, or until the sauce has thickened slightly.
11. Season with pepper to taste.
12. Strain the prepared pasta and combine with the sauce in the pan.
13. Shake or toss everything together until the pasta is well coated with the sauce.
14. Serve the pasta hot, topped with grated Parmesan cheese and garnished with fresh parsley.

2. Fettuccine with Clam Sauce

Ingredients:
- 1 pound fettuccine pasta
- 2 pounds fresh clams
- 2 tablespoons olive oil
- 4 garlic cloves, minced
- 1/4 teaspoon red pepper flakes
- 1/2 cup dry white wine
- 1 cup chicken broth
- 1/2 cup heavy cream
- 2 tablespoons chopped fresh parsley
- Salt and pepper to taste

Instructions:
1. Fill a sizable pot with four quarts of H20 [water] and bring to a rolling boil.
2. Add two tablespoons of salt to the boiling water.
3. Add one pound of fettuccine to the pot and stir occasionally to prevent clumping.
4. Prepare the fettuccine until it becomes firm or al dente, which means it should be tender but still firm to the bite. Fresh fettuccine typically takes about two to three minutes to cook, while dried fettuccine may take up to eight minutes. Reserve one cup or bowl of pasta water and drain the rest.
5. While the pasta is cooking, rinse the clams and remove any sand or dirt. Discard any clams that are open and do not close when tapped.
6. In a large saucepan, heat the olive oil over moderatetemperature. Add the chopped red pepper flakes and garlic and cook until fragrant, about one minute.
7. Add the wine to the pan and bring to a boil. Cook for two to three minutes, until the liquid has reduced by half.
8. Put the clams in the pot, cover tightly, and cook for two to three minutes, until the clams have opened. Discard any clams that have not opened.
9. Remove the clams from the pan and set aside. Keep the liquid in the pan.
10. Put the chicken stock in the pot and bring to a boil. Cook for two to three minutes, until the liquid has reduced by half.
11. Stir in the heavy cream and return the clams to the pan. Cook for two to three minutes, until the sauce has thickened slightly.
12. In case the sauce is very thick, put in some of the reserved pasta H20 [water] to thin it out.
13. Toss the cooked fettuccine with the sauce and the chopped parsley. Season with salt and pepper to taste. Serve hot.

4.2. FETTUCCINE

3. Fettuccine with Shrimp Scampi

Ingredients:
- 1 pound fettuccine pasta
- 1/2 cup unsalted butter
- 6 cloves of garlic, minced
- 1 pound large shrimp, peeled and deveined
- 1/4 cup white wine
- 2 tablespoons lemon juice
- 1/2 teaspoon red pepper flakes
- Salt and pepper to taste
- Fresh parsley for garnish

Instructions:
1. Fill a sizable saucepan with four quarts of H20 [water] and bring to a rolling boil.
2. Add two tablespoons of salt to the boiling water.
3. Add one pound of fettuccine to the pot and stir occasionally to prevent clumping.
4. Prepare the fettuccine until it becomes firm or al dente, which means it should be tender but still firm to the bite. Fresh fettuccine typically takes about two to three minutes to cook, while dried fettuccine may take up to eight minutes.
5. In a sizable skillet, liquefy the butter over moderatetemperature.
6. Add the chopped-up garlic and prepare until fragrant, approximately thirty seconds.
7. Put the shrimp into the pot and cook until pink, about two minutes per side.
8. Add the white wine, lemon juice, red pepper flakes, salt and pepper to the pan.
9. Control the mixture until it boils and let it bubble for two to three minutes maximum.
10. Strain the prepared pasta and put it into the pot with the sauce.
11. Shake or toss everything together until the pasta is well coated with the sauce.
12. Serve the pasta hot, garnished with fresh parsley.

4. Fettuccine with Mushroom Sauce

Ingredients:
- 1 pound fettuccine pasta
- 1 tablespoon olive oil
- 1/2 cup diced onions
- 2 cloves of garlic, minced
- 8 ounces sliced mushrooms
- 1/2 cup white wine
- 1 cup heavy cream
- Salt and pepper to taste

Instructions:

1. Fill a sizable saucepan with four quarts of H2O [water] and bring to a rolling boil.
2. Add two tablespoons of salt to the boiling water.
3. Add one pound of fettuccine to the pot and stir occasionally to prevent clumping.
4. Prepare the fettuccine till it becomes al dente, which means it should be tender but still firm to the bite. Fresh fettuccine typically takes about two to three minutes to cook, while dried fettuccine may take up to eight minutes.
5. In a separate saucepan, heat the olive oil over medium heat. Add the diced onions and cook until softened, about five minutes.
6. Add the minced garlic and sliced mushrooms to the saucepan and continue to cook until the mushrooms are tender, about five to seven minutes.
7. Deglaze the saucepan with the white wine, scraping any browned bits off the bottom of the pan. Reduce the wine until it is almost completely evaporated.
8. Whisk in the heavy cream and increase flavour with salt and pepper to taste. Simmer the sauce until it has thickened slightly, about five minutes.
9. Reserve one cup or bowl of the pasta cooking H20 [water], then with a strainer, drain the pasta and add it to the saucepan with the sauce. Toss to coat the pasta evenly.
10. In case the sauce is very thick, put in some of the reserved pasta cooking H20 [water] to achieve the desired consistency.
11. Serve the fettuccine with mushroom sauce hot.

4.2. FETTUCCINE

5. Fettuccine Alfredo

Ingredients:
- 1 pound fettuccine pasta
- 1 cup heavy cream
- 1 cup grated Parmesan cheese
- 4 tablespoons unsalted butter
- Salt and pepper to taste

Instructions:
1. Fill a sizable saucepan with four quarts of H2O [water] and bring to a rolling boil.
2. Add two tablespoons of salt to the boiling water.
3. Add one pound of fettuccine to the pot and stir occasionally to prevent clumping.
4. Prepare the fettuccine until it becomes firm or al dente, which means it should be tender but still firm to the bite. Fresh fettuccine typically takes about two to three minutes to cook, while dried fettuccine may take up to eight minutes.
5. In a separate saucepan, heat the heavy cream over moderate heat until it starts to bubble.
6. Turn down the heat to very low and put the grated Parmesan cheese, stirring continuously until the cheese is melted and the mixture is smooth.
7. Stir in the unsalted butter and season with salt and pepper to taste.
8. Reserve a single cup or bowl of the pasta cooking H20 [water], then using a strainer, drain the pasta and add it to the saucepan with the sauce. Toss to coat the pasta evenly.
9. In case the sauce is very thick, put in some of the reserved pasta cooking H20 [water] to achieve the desired consistency.
10. Serve the fettuccine Alfredo hot with additional grated Parmesan cheese, if desired.

4.3. LINGUINE

1. Linguine with Clams

Ingredients:
- 1 pound linguine pasta
- 2 poundsclams, washed and scrubbed
- 4 cloves garlic, minced
- 1/2 cup white wine
- 1/4 cup olive oil
- 1/4 teaspoon red pepper flakes (optional)
- Salt and pepper to taste
- 2 tablespoons chopped fresh parsley

Instructions:
1. Fill a sizable pot with four quarts of H20 [water] and bring to a rolling boil
2. Add two tablespoons of salt to the boiling water.
3. Add one pound of linguine to the pot and stir occasionally to prevent clumping.
4. Prepare the linguine till it becomes firm or al dente, which means it should be tender but still firm to the bite. Fresh linguine typically takes about two to three minutes to cook, while dried linguine may take up to eight minutes. Reserve one cup of pasta water.
5. In a sizable saucepan over moderate temperature, heat the olive oil and add garlic. Cook for one minute until fragrant.
6. Add the clams and white wine to the pan. Cover and cook for five minutes or until the clams open. Discard any unopened clams.
7. Add the salt, pepper, and red pepper flakes to the pan and stir.
8. Drain the linguine and add it to the pan with the clams. Toss to combine and add some pasta water to loosen the sauce if necessary.
9. Serve the linguine with clams immediately, topped with chopped parsley.

2. Linguine with Tomato and Basil Sauce

Ingredients:
- 1 pound linguine pasta
- 1/4 cup olive oil
- 4 cloves garlic, minced
- 1 can (14.5 ounces) diced tomatoes
- 1/4 teaspoon sugar
- Salt and pepper to taste
- 1/2 cup fresh basil leaves, torn
- 1/4 cup freshly grated Parmesan cheese

Instructions:
1. Fill a sizable pot with four quarts of H20 [water] and bring to a rolling boil.
2. Add two tablespoons of salt to the boiling water.
3. Add one pound of linguine to the pot and stir occasionally to prevent clumping.
4. Prepare the linguine till it becomes firm or al dente, which means it should be tender but still firm to the bite. Fresh linguine typically takes about two to three minutes to cook, while dried linguine may take up to eight minutes. Reserve one cup of pasta water.
5. In a sizable saucepan over moderate temperature, heat the olive oil and add garlic. Cook for one minute until fragrant.
6. Add the diced tomatoes, sugar, salt, and pepper to the pan. Boil for ten minutes or until the sauce is completely thick.
7. Stir in the torn basil leaves.
8. Drain the linguine and add it to the pan with the tomato sauce. Toss to combine and add some pasta water to loosen the sauce if necessary.
9. Serve the linguine with tomato and basil sauce immediately, topped with grated Parmesan cheese.

4.3. LINGUINE

4. Linguine with Garlic and Oil

Ingredients:
- 1 pound linguine
- 1/2 cup olive oil
- 8 cloves garlic, minced
- Salt and pepper to taste
- 1/4 cup chopped fresh parsley

Instructions:
1. Fill a sizable pot with four quarts of H20 [water] and bring to a rolling boil.
2. Add two tablespoons of salt to the boiling water.
3. Add one pound of linguine to the pot and stir occasionally to prevent clumping.
4. Prepare the linguine till it becomes firm or al dente, which means it should be tender but still firm to the bite. Fresh linguine typically takes about two to three minutes to cook, while dried linguine may take up to eight minutes. Reserve one cup of the pasta water. Drain the pasta and keep by the side.
5. In a sizable skillet, warm the olive oil over medium temperature. Add the minced garlic and cook for two minutes until fragrant.
6. Add the cooked linguine to the skillet and toss to coat with the garlic oil. In case the sauce is very thick, put in some of the reserved pasta water to help thin it out.
7. Season the linguine with salt and pepper to taste.
8. Serve the linguine hot, garnished with chopped parsley and additional olive oil if desired.

3. Linguine with Spinach and Ricotta

Ingredients:
- 1 pound linguine
- 2 tablespoons olive oil
- 3 cloves garlic, minced
- 4 cups spinach, washed and chopped
- 1 cup ricotta cheese
- 1/2 cup grated Parmesan cheese
- Salt and pepper to taste

Instructions:
1. Fill a sizable pot with four quarts of H20 [water] and bring to a rolling boil.
2. Add two tablespoons of salt to the boiling water.
3. Add one pound of linguine to the pot and stir occasionally to prevent clumping.
4. Prepare the linguine till it becomes firm or al dente, which means it should be tender but still

firm to the bite. Fresh linguine typically takes about two to three minutes to cook, while dried linguine may take up to eight minutes. Reserve one cup of the pasta water. Drain the pasta and keep by the side.

5. In a sizable skillet, warm the olive oil over medium temperature. Add the minced garlic and cook for two minutes until fragrant.

6. Combine the minced spinach with the skillet and prepare for two minutes until wilted.

7. Stir in the ricotta cheese, grated Parmesan cheese, salt, and pepper. Cook for two minutes until the cheese has melted and the sauce has thickened.

8. Add the cooked linguine to the skillet and toss to coat with the sauce. In case the sauce is very thick, put in some of the reserved pasta water to help thin it out.

9. Serve the linguine hot, garnished with additional Parmesan cheese if desired.

5. Linguine with Mussels

Ingredients:
- 1 pound linguine
- 2 poundsmussels, cleaned and debearded
- 4 cloves of garlic, minced
- 1 cup white wine
- 1/4 cup olive oil
- Salt and pepper to taste
- 1/4 cup chopped fresh parsley

Instructions:
1. Fill a sizable pot with four quarts of H20 [water] and bring to a rolling boil.
2. Add two tablespoons of salt to the boiling water.
3. Add one pound of linguine to the pot and stir occasionally to prevent clumping.
4. Prepare the linguine till it becomes firm or al dente, which means it should be tender but still firm to the bite. Fresh linguine typically takes about two to three minutes to cook, while dried linguine may take up to eight minutes.
5. In a sizable skillet, warm the olive oil over medium temperature. Add garlic and cook until fragrant, about one to two minutes.
6. Add mussels to the pan and pour in white wine. Cover the pot tightly with a lid and continue to cook for five to seven minutes, until the mussels have opened. Discard any mussels that do not open.
7. Drain the linguine and add it to the pan with the mussels. Toss the linguine and mussels together until the sauce has coated the pasta evenly.
8. Season with salt and pepper to taste.
9. Serve in bowls, topped with chopped parsley.

4.4. LASAGNA

1. Classic Meat Lasagna

Ingredients:
- 1 pound ground beef or ground turkey
- 1 large onion, chopped
- 4 garlic cloves, minced
- 2 cans (14.5 ounces each) of crushed tomatoes
- 2 tablespoons tomato paste
- 1 teaspoon dried basil
- 1 teaspoon dried oregano
- Salt and black pepper, to taste
- 9 lasagna noodles
- 15 ounces of ricotta cheese
- 2 large eggs
- 1/2 cup grated Parmesan cheese
- 4 cups shredded mozzarella cheese

Instructions:
1. Preheat oven to 375°F.
2. In a sizable pot over medium temperature, cook the ground beef or turkey and onion until browned, about ten minutes.
3. Add the chopped garlic and prepare for an additional two minutes.
4. Whisk in the basil, chopped tomatoes, salt, tomato paste, oregano, pepper and oregano.
5. Steam for twenty minutes, stirring occasionally.
6. Fill a sizable saucepan with four quarts of H2O [water] and bring to a rolling boil.
7. Add two tablespoons of salt to the boiling water.
8. Add lasagna noodles to the boiling water, making sure they are fully submerged.
9. Fresh noodles typically take about four to five minutes to cook, while dried noodles may take up to ten minutes.
10. Rinse and drain the noodles with very cold water to bring the cooking process to a halt and prevent sticking.
11. In a different dish, combine together the eggs, Parmesan cheese and ricotta cheese.
12. In a 9x13-inch baking bowl, spread a layer of the meat sauce on the very bottom.
13. Place three lasagna noodles on the very top of the meat sauce.
14. Spread a layer of the ricotta mixture over the noodles.
15. Top with a layer of the fantastic mozzarella cheese.
16. Repeat the layers, ending with a layer of mozzarella.
17. Bake for twenty-five minutes with the baking dish covered in aluminum foil.

18. Take off the foil and continue baking for another twenty minutes, till the cheese is completely melted and bubbling.
19. Allow the lasagna to cool for ten minutes before serving.

2. Spinach and Ricotta Lasagna

Ingredients:
- 12 lasagna noodles
- 1 large egg, beaten
- 15 ounces ricotta cheese
- 1 1/2 cups shredded mozzarella cheese
- 1/2 cup grated Parmesan cheese
- 2 cloves garlic, minced
- 1/2 teaspoon salt
- 1/4 teaspoon black pepper
- 10 ounces frozen chopped spinach, thawed and drained
- 1 jar of marinara sauce

Instructions:
1. Preheat oven to 375°F.
2. Fill a sizable pot with four quarts of H20 [water] and bring to a rolling boil.
3. Add two tablespoons of salt to the boiling water.
4. Add lasagna noodles to the boiling water, making sure they are fully submerged.
5. Fresh noodles typically take about four to five minutes to cook, while dried noodles may take up to ten minutes.
6. Rinse and drain the noodles with very cold water in other to bring the cooking process to a halt and prevent sticking.
7. In a large bowl, mix together the egg, ricotta cheese, 1 cup of mozzarella cheese, Parmesan cheese, garlic, salt, and pepper.
8. Stir in the spinach until well combined.
9. Spread a thin layer of marinara sauce on the very bottom of a 9 by13 inch size baking bowl.
10. Place three lasagna noodles on the very top of the made sauce.
11. Spread 1/3 of the cheese and spinach mixture on top of the noodles.
12. Repeat layering two more times, ending with a layer of marinara sauce on top.
13. Sprinkle the remaining 1/2 cup of mozzarella cheese on top.
14. Cover with aluminium paper and bake for approximately thirty minutes.
15. Remove aluminium paper and bake for an additional fifteen to twenty minutes maximum or until the cheese is completely melted and it is bubbling.
16. Allow the lasagna to chill for ten to fifteen minutes before slicing and serving.

4.4. LASAGNA

3. Seafood Lasagna

Ingredients:
- 12 lasagna noodles
- 3 tablespoons olive oil
- 1 onion, chopped
- 3 cloves of garlic, minced
- 1 cup heavy cream
- 1 cup chicken broth
- 1/2 teaspoon dried basil
- 1/2 teaspoon dried oregano
- 1/4 teaspoon red pepper flakes
- Salt and pepper, to taste
- 1 pound mixed seafood (such as shrimp, scallops, and crab meat), thawed and drained
- 1 cup grated Parmesan cheese
- 1 cup shredded mozzarella cheese
- Fresh parsley, chopped (optional, for garnish)

Instructions:
1. Fill a sizable pan with four quarts of H2O [water] and bring to a rolling boil.
2. Add two tablespoons of salt to the boiling water.
3. Add lasagna noodles to the boiling water, making sure they are fully submerged.
4. Fresh noodles typically take about four to five minutes to cook, while dried noodles may take up to ten minutes.
5. Rinse and drain the noodles with very cold water to bring the cooking process to a halt and prevent sticking.
6. In a sizable dish, heat the olive oil over medium temperature. Add the minced onion and prepare until it is really soft, for about five minutes.
7. Add the minced garlic and cook for another minute.
8. Pour in the heavy cream, chicken broth, dried basil, salt, oregano, pepper, and red pepper flakes. Beat to mix.
9. Gently bring the combination to a rolling boil and cook for about ten minutes, until the sauce has thickened slightly.
10. Stir in the mixed seafood and cook until just heated through, about five minutes.
11. Preheat the cooker\oven to 375°F. Grease a 9x13 inch baking dish.
12. To assemble the lasagna, spread a thin layer of the seafood mixture on the bottom of the baking bowl.
13. Cover the mixture with a coat of lasagna noodles.
14. Sprinkle a layer of grated Parmesan cheese over the noodles.

15. Repeat the layering process (seafood mixture, noodles, Parmesan cheese) two more times.
16. Sprinkle the chopped mozzarella cheese on top of the final level of noodles.
17. Bake for at least twenty-five minutes with the baking dish covered with foil.
18. Remove the aluminum foil and continue baking for ten to fifteen minutes, or till the cheese is completely melted and bubbling.
19. Set aside for a couple of minutes before dividing and serving the lasagna. Garnish with fresh parsley, if desired. Enjoy!

4. Chicken Alfredo Lasagna

Ingredients:
- 1 pound skinless, boneless chicken breast, sliced into tiny cubes
- 1 cup heavy cream
- 1 cup grated Parmesan cheese
- 1 cup grated mozzarella cheese
- 1/4 teaspoon garlic powder
- Salt and pepper to taste
- 1 pound lasagna noodles
- 2 cups Alfredo sauce

Instructions:
1. Preheat oven to 375°F.
2. In a large saucepan, cook chicken cubes over medium heat until browned and fully cooked. Set aside.
3. In another saucepan, heat the heavy cream over low heat until it begins to simmer. Stir in Parmesan cheese, mozzarella cheese, garlic powder, salt, and pepper.
4. Fill a sizable pan with four quarts of H2O [water] and bring to a rolling boil.
5. Add two tablespoons of salt to the boiling water.
6. Add lasagna noodles to the boiling water, making sure they are fully submerged.
7. Fresh noodles typically take about four to five minutes to cook, while dried noodles may take up to ten minutes.
8. Rinse and drain the noodles with very cold water to bring the cooking process to a halt and prevent sticking.
9. In a 9 by 13-inch size baking bowl, sprinkle a coat of Alfredo dip\sauce on the very bottom of the bowl.
10. Layer lasagna noodles over the sauce, followed by another layer of Alfredo sauce, chicken cubes, and the cheese mixture. Repeat the layering until all ingredients are used up, making sure to end with a layer of cheese mixture on the top.
11. Bake for at least twenty-five minutes with the baking pan covered in aluminum foil. Remove the aluminum foil and continue baking for another ten to fifteen minutes, till the cheese has melted and turned golden brown.
12. Serve hot and enjoy your delicious Chicken Alfredo Lasagna!

4.5. TORTELLINI

1. Cheese Tortellini

Ingredients:

- 2 cups all-purpose flour
- 3 large eggs
- 1/2 teaspoon salt
- 1 cup ricotta cheese
- 1/2 cup grated Parmesan cheese
- 1/2 teaspoon freshly ground black pepper

Instructions:

1. In a sizable bowl, stir together the salt and flour.
2. In another bowl, beat the eggs.
3. Pour the beaten eggs into the flour mixture and stir until a smooth dough forms.
4. Empty the ball of dough out onto a lightly floured surfaceand work for about five to seven minutes, or until smooth and elastic.
5. Seal the dough with plastic wrap and allow it to settle for about thirty minutes.
6. For the time being, in a sizable dish, stir together the ricotta cheese, Parmesan cheese, and black pepper.
7. Spread the dough out on a floured surface to about 1/8-inch thickness.
8. Cut the dough into two- to three-inch circles.
9. Place a small spoonful of the cheese filling in the center of each circle.
10. Fold the circle in half to form a half-moon shape, pressing the edges together to seal.
11. Bring a big pot of water that has been salted to a boil.
12. Prepare the tortellini for about three to five minutes, or until they float to the surface.
13. Serve with your favorite sauce and sprinkle with grated Parmesan cheese.

2. Chicken Tortellini

Ingredients:

- 1 pound fresh pasta dough
- 2 boneless, skinless chicken breasts, diced into small pieces
- 1 cup ricotta cheese
- 1 egg
- 1 cup grated Parmesan cheese
- 1 teaspoon dried basil
- 1 teaspoon dried oregano
- Salt and pepper, to taste
- 2 quarts of water
- 2 tablespoons olive oil
- Fresh chopped parsley, for garnish (optional)

Instructions:

1. Start by making the pasta dough. Combine flour and egg in a large mixing bowl. Gradually add water and mix until the dough forms a smooth ball. Knead the dough for eight to ten minutes, wrap it in plastic wrap and allow it to settle for about thirty minutes.

2. In a saucepan, heat olive oil over medium temperature. Add chicken and cook for about six to eight minutes, or until browned and cooked through. Season with salt and pepper.

3. In a mixing bowl, combine the cooked chicken, ricotta cheese, egg, Parmesan cheese, basil, oregano, and a pinch of salt and pepper. Mix until well combined.

4. Roll out the pasta dough on a moderately floured surface to a desired thickness of approximately 1/8 inch. Slice the pasta into two-inch circles using a cookie cutter or a glass.

5. Place a small spoonful of the chicken mixture in the center of each pasta circle. Fold the circle in half, sealing the edges together. Bend the ends towards each other and overlap, forming the shape of a tortellini. Repeat with the remaining pasta circles and chicken mixture.

6. Bring a large pot of salted water to a boil. Put the tortellini into the pot of boiling water and let it cook for about three to four minutes, or until they float to the surface.

7. Drain the tortellini and serve with your favorite sauce, or just with a drizzle of olive oil and some freshly grated Parmesan cheese. Sprinkle with fresh chopped parsley, if desired.

8. Enjoy your delicious homemade chicken tortellini!

4.5. TORTELLINI

3. Spinach and Ricotta Tortellini

Ingredients:
- 2 cups all-purpose flour
- 2 large eggs
- 1/2 cup freshly grated Parmesan cheese
- 1/2 teaspoon salt
- 1/2 teaspoon freshly ground black pepper
- 2 cups fresh spinach, blanched and chopped
- 1 cup ricotta cheese
- One egg yolk, mixed with a small amount of water to form an egg wash.

Instructions:
1. In a sizable mixing dish, put together the salt, flour, eggs, Parmesan cheese, and pepper. Mix with your hands until the dough comes together in a ball. Work the dough on a moderately floured surface for about ten minutes maximum until soft and elastic. Cover the bowl of dough in plastic wrap and allow it to settle for approximately thirty minutes.
2. In a separate bowl, combine the chopped spinach and ricotta cheese. Season with salt and pepper to taste.
3. Roll out the dough into thin sheets on a floured surface. Cut the sheets into three-inch circles. Place a small spoonful of the spinach and ricotta mixture in the center of each circle.
4. Fold the flattened dough well over the filling to create a half-moon shape and hold down all the edges to seal. Fold the two ends of the half-moon towards each other and press them together to form a tortellini shape.
5. Boil the tortellini in salted water for about three to four minutes, or until they float to the surface. Serve with your favorite sauce.

4. Mushroom and Herb Tortellini

Ingredients:
- 2 cups all-purpose flour
- 2 large eggs
- 1/2 cup freshly grated Parmesan cheese
- 1/2 teaspoon salt
- 1/2 teaspoon freshly ground black pepper
- 2 cups finely chopped mushrooms
- 1/4 cup chopped fresh herbs (such as basil, parsley, or thyme)
- 1 cup ricotta cheese
- One egg yolk, mixed with a small amount of water to form an egg wash

Instructions:

1. In a sizable mixing dish, put together the salt, flour, eggs, Parmesan cheese, and pepper. Mix with your hands until the dough comes together in a ball. Work the dough on a moderately floured surface for about ten minutes, maximum until soft and elastic. Cover the bowl of dough in plastic wrap and allow it to settle for approximately thirty minutes.

2. In a separate bowl, combine the chopped mushrooms, herbs, and ricotta cheese. Season with salt and pepper to taste.

3. Roll out the dough into thin sheets on a floured surface. Cut the sheets into three-inch circles. Place a small spoonful of the mushroom and herb mixture in the center of each circle.

4. Fold the flattened dough well over the filling to create a half-moon shape and hold down all the edges to seal. Fold the two ends of the half-moon towards each other and press them together to form a tortellini shape.

5. Boil the tortellini in salted water for about three to four minutes, or until they float to the surface. Serve with your favorite sauce.

4.5. TORTELLINI

5. Beef Tortellini

Ingredients:
- 2 cups all-purpose flour
- 3 large eggs
- 1/2 teaspoon salt
- 1 poundground beef
- 1/2 cup diced onions
- 1/2 cup diced carrots
- 1/2 cup diced celery
- 2 cloves garlic, minced
- 1/2 teaspoon dried basil
- 1/2 teaspoon dried oregano
- 1/2 teaspoon dried thyme
- Salt and pepper to taste

Instructions:
1. In a sizable bowl, stir together the salt and flour.
2. In another bowl, beat the eggs.
3. Pour the beaten eggs into the flour mixture and stir until a smooth dough forms.
4. Pour the ball of dough out onto a gently floured surface and work for about five to seven minutes, or until smooth and elastic.
5. Seal the dough with plastic wrap and allow it to settle for about thirty minutes.
6. Meanwhile, in a sizable skillet over medium temperature, cook the ground beef until browned. Drain any excess fat.
7. Add the onions, carrots, celery, and garlic to the skillet and cook until the vegetables are soft and fragrant, about five minutes.
8. Stir in the basil, oregano, thyme, salt, and pepper.
9. Remove from heat and let the filling cool.
10. Spread the dough out on a floured surface to about 1/8 inch thickness.
11. Cut the dough into two- to three-inch circles.
12. Place a small spoonful of the beef filling in the center of each circle.
13. Fold the circle in half to form a half-moon shape, pressing the edges together to seal.
14. Bring a big pot of water that has been salted to a boil.
15. Prepare the tortellini for about three to five minutes, or until they float to the surface.
16. Serve with your favorite sauce and sprinkle with grated Parmesan cheese.

4.6. GNOCCHI

1. Potato Gnocchi

Ingredients:
- 2 pounds large potatoes, peeled and boiled
- 2 cups all-purpose flour
- 1 large egg
- Salt, to taste

Instructions:
1. Mash the boiled potatoes in a bowl, making sure they are smooth and free of lumps.
2. Add in the flour and egg, and mix until a dough forms.
3. Knead the ball of dough on a lightly floured surfaceuntil smooth, about three to five minutes.
4. Roll the dough into long tubes, about the size of a pencil, and cut into small pieces, about one-inch long.
5. Roll each piece of dough over the tines of a fork, pressing down slightly to create ridges.
6. Boil the gnocchi in salted water for about two to three minutes, or until they float to the top.
7. Serve the gnocchi with your favorite sauce or toppings.

2. Spinach Gnocchi

Ingredients:
- 2 pounds large potatoes, peeled and boiled
- 1 cup fresh spinach leaves
- 2 cups all-purpose flour
- 1 large egg
- Salt, to taste
- Nutmeg, to taste

Instructions:
1. Mash the boiled potatoes in a bowl, making sure they are smooth and free of lumps.
2. Add in the fresh spinach leaves and blend together until the spinach is fully incorporated into the mashed potatoes.
3. Add in the flour, egg, salt, and nutmeg, and mix until a dough forms.
4. Knead the ball of dough on a lightly floured surfaceuntil smooth, about three to five minutes.
5. Roll the dough into long tubes, about the size of a pencil, and cut into small pieces, about

one-inch long.

6. Roll each piece of dough over the tines of a fork, pressing down slightly to create ridges.
7. Boil the gnocchi in salted water for about two to three minutes, or until they float to the top.
8. Serve the gnocchi with your favorite sauce or toppings.

3. Sweet Potato Gnocchi

Ingredients:
- 2 pounds sweet potatoes
- 2 cups all-purpose flour
- 2 large eggs
- 1 teaspoon salt
- 1 teaspoon nutmeg

Instructions:
1. Boil the sweet potatoes in salted water until they are soft, then drain and let cool.
2. Crush the sweetpotatoes in a sizable dish and add the flour, eggs, salt, and nutmeg. Mix until a dough forms.
3. Knead the ball of dough for approximately five minutes until smooth, then roll it into one-inch thick ropes. Cut the ropes into one-inch pieces.
4. Turn every piece [1-inch] of dough into a unique ball, then use a fork to press down and make ridges on each gnocchi.
5. Boil the gnocchi in salted water for about two to three minutes, or until they float to the surface.
6. Serve with your favorite sauce or toppings.

4.6. GNOCCHI

4. Tomato Gnocchi

Ingredients:
- 2 cups all-purpose flour
- 1 cup tomato puree
- 2 large eggs
- 1 teaspoon salt
- 1 teaspoon basil
- 1 teaspoon oregano

Instructions:
1. In a sizable mixing dish, mix together the salt, flour, tomato puree, eggs, salt, basil, and oregano until a dough forms.
2. Knead the ball of dough for approximately five minutes until smooth, then roll it into one-inch thick ropes. Cut the ropes into one-inch pieces.
3. Turn every piece [one-inch] of dough into a unique ball, then use a fork to press down and make ridges on each gnocchi.
4. Boil the gnocchi in salted water for about two to three minutes, or until they float to the surface.
5. Serve with your favorite sauce or toppings.

5. Pumpkin Gnocchi

Ingredients:
- 2 cups all-purpose flour
- 1 cup cooked pumpkin puree
- 2 large eggs
- 1 teaspoon salt
- 1 teaspoon nutmeg
- 1 teaspoon cinnamon

Instructions:
1. In a sizable mixing dish, mix together the salt, flour, tomato puree, eggs, salt, basil, and oregano until a dough forms.
2. Knead the ball of dough for approximately five minutes until smooth, then roll it into one-inch thick ropes. Cut the ropes into one-inch pieces.
3. Turn every piece [one-inch] of dough into a unique ball, then use a fork to press down and make ridges on each gnocchi.
4. Boil the gnocchi in salted water for about two to three minutes, or until they float to the surface.
5. Serve with your favorite sauce or toppings.

4.7. PAPPARDELLE

1. Pappardelle with Shrimp Scampi

Ingredients:

- 1 pound pappardelle pasta
- 1 pound large shrimp, peeled and deveined
- 4 clovesof garlic, minced
- 1/4 cup white wine
- 2 tablespoons lemon juice
- 2 tablespoons unsalted butter
- Salt and pepper to taste
- 2 tablespoons chopped fresh parsley (optional)

Instructions:

1. Fill a sizable saucepan with water and boil it over high heat.
2. Add salt to the boiling water, around one teaspoon per quart of water.
3. Slowly add the pappardelle pasta to the pot, stirring gently to prevent sticking.
4. Cook the pasta for about two to four minutes, or until it reaches an al dente texture.
5. Test the pasta by taking a strand and biting it. If it is firm but not crunchy, it's done. If not, cook for another minute and check again.
6. Drain the pasta in a colander and wash it with very cold water to bring the cooking process to a halt.
7. In a large skillet, heat two tablespoons of butter over medium heat.
8. Stir in the minced garlic and simmer for approximately a minute, or until fragrant.
9. Stir in the shrimp and sauté them in the skillet for two to three minutes, or until they turn pink.
10. Add the lemon juice and white wine, then mix.Season with salt and pepper to taste.
11. Drain the pappardelle pasta and add it to the shrimp scampi sauce.
12. Toss until the pasta is fully coated with the sauce.
13. Serve with a sprinkle of chopped parsley if desired.

2. Pappardelle with Bolognese Sauce

Ingredients:

- 1 pound pappardelle pasta
- 2 tablespoons olive oil
- 1 medium onion, chopped
- 2 garlic cloves, minced
- 1 poundground beef
- 1 cup red wine
- 2 cans (14.5 ounces each) diced tomatoes
- Salt and black pepper, to taste
- Fresh basil leaves, for garnish

Instructions:

1. Fill a sizable saucepan with water and boil it over high heat.
2. Add salt to the boiling water, around one teaspoon per quart of water.
3. Slowly add the pappardelle pasta to the pot, stirring gently to prevent sticking.
4. Cook the pasta for about two to four minutes, or until it reaches an al dente texture.
5. Test the pasta by taking a strand and biting it. If it is firm but not crunchy, it's done. If not, cook for another minute and check again.
6. Drain the pasta in a colander and wash it with very cold water to bring the cooking process to a halt.
7. In a large saucepan, heat olive oil over medium temperature.
8. Add the minced garlic and onion and prepare until it becomes very soft, for about five minutes.
9. Put the ground beef in the saucepan and cook until totally browned, while using a wooden spoon to break up the beef.
10. Pour in the red wine and let it cook for about two minutes.
11. Stir in the diced tomatoes and let the sauce simmer for about ten minutes, until thickened.
12. Sprinkle the sauce with pepper and salt to taste.
13. Dish the cooked pappardelle with the bolognese sauce on top.
14. Garnish with fresh basil leaves and enjoy!

4.7. PAPPARDELLE

3. Pappardelle with Chicken and Asparagus

Ingredients:

- 8 ounces of fresh pappardelle pasta
- Two skinless, boneless chicken breasts, sliced into 1-inch size pieces
- One bunch of asparagus, trimmed and cut into 1-inch pieces
- 2 tablespoons of olive oil

- 2 cloves of garlic, minced
- 1/2 teaspoon of dried basil
- 1/2 teaspoon of dried oregano
- Salt and pepper to taste
- 1/2 cup of chicken broth
- 1/2 cup of heavy cream
- 1/2 cup of freshly grated Parmesan cheese

Instructions:

1. Fill a sizable saucepan with water and boil it over high heat.
2. Add salt to the boiling water, around one teaspoon per quart of water.
3. Slowly add the pappardelle pasta to the pot, stirring gently to prevent sticking.
4. Cook the pasta for about two to four minutes, or until it reaches an al dente texture.
5. Test the pasta by taking a strand and biting it. If it is firm but not crunchy, it's done. If not, cook for another minute and check again.
6. Drain the pasta in a colander and wash it with very cold water to bring the cooking process to a halt.
7. In a large saucepan, heat olive oil over medium temperature. Add the chicken pieces and cook for about six to eight minutes or until browned on all sides and cooked thoroughly.
8. Take out the chicken from the pot and place it to the side. Put the asparagus and prepare for approximately three to four minutes or until tender. Remove the asparagus from the skillet and set aside.
9. In the same skillet, add the garlic, basil, oregano, salt, and pepper. Cook for one to two minutes or until fragrant.
10. Add the heavy cream and chicken stock to the skillet and stir to combine. Bring to a boil, reduce heat to low, and let simmer for five minutes or until the sauce has thickened.
11. Return the chicken and asparagus to the skillet and stir to combine with the sauce.
12. Serve the chicken and asparagus mixture over the cooked pappardelle pasta. Sprinkle with freshly grated Parmesan cheese. Serve and enjoy!

4. Pappardelle with Mushroom Sauce

Ingredients:
- 1 pound fresh pappardelle pasta
- 2 tablespoons olive oil
- 1 large onion, chopped
- 4 clovesof garlic, minced
- 8 ounces sliced mushrooms

- 2 cups chicken or vegetable broth
- 1/2 cup heavy cream
- 1/4 cup grated Parmesan cheese
- Salt and pepper to taste
- Fresh parsley for garnish

Instructions:
1. Fill a sizable saucepan with water and boil it over high heat.
2. Add salt to the boiling water, around one teaspoon per quart of water.
3. Slowly add the pappardelle pasta to the pot, stirring gently to prevent sticking.
4. Cook the pasta for about two to four minutes, or until it reaches an al dente texture.
5. Test the pasta by taking a strand and biting it. If it is firm but not crunchy, it's done. If not, cook for another minute and check again.
6. Drain the pasta in a colander and wash it with very cold water to bring the cooking process to a halt.
7. In a large saucepan, heat olive oil over medium temperature.
8. Add the chopped onion and minced garlic to the skillet and cook until softened, about three to five minutes.
9. Put the chopped mushrooms into the pot and continue to cook until they are tender and have released their moisture, about five to seven minutes.
10. Throw in the veggie or chicken broth and bring to a simmer. Let cook for two to three minutes, until the broth has reduced slightly.
11. Whisk in the shredded Parmesan cheese and the heavy cream, and continue to cook until the sauce has thickened, about two to three minutes.
12. Season the sauce with salt and pepper to taste.
13. Toss the cooked pappardelle pasta with the mushroom sauce, until well coated.
14. Serve the pappardelle with mushroom sauce hot, garnished with fresh parsley if desired. Enjoy!

5. Pappardelle with Roasted Tomato Sauce

Ingredients:
- 1 pound pappardelle pasta
- 4 large ripe tomatoes, diced
- 1 tablespoon olive oil
- 4 clovesof garlic, minced
- 1/2 teaspoon dried oregano
- Salt and pepper to taste
- 2 tablespoons chopped fresh basil (optional)

Instructions:
1. Preheat oven to 400°F.
2. Spread the diced tomatoes on a baking sheet and drizzle with one tablespoon of olive oil.
3. Bake the tomatoes for twenty minutes in the oven.
4. Fill a big saucepan with fresh water and boil on high heat.
5. Add salt to the boiling water, around one teaspoon per quart of water.
6. Slowly add the pappardelle pasta to the pot, stirring gently to prevent sticking.
7. Cook the pasta for about two to four minutes, or until it reaches an al dente texture.
8. Test the pasta by taking a strand and biting it. If it is firm but not crunchy, it's done. If not, cook for another minute and check again.
9. Drain the pasta in a colander and wash it with very cold water to bring the cooking process to a halt.
10. In a big pot, heat one tablespoon of olive oil over medium heat.
11. Add chopped garlic to the saucepan and cook until fragrant, about one minute.
12. Add the roasted tomatoes to the skillet and stir to combine.
13. Season with dried oregano, salt, and pepper to taste.
14. Drain the pappardelle pasta and add it to the tomato sauce.
15. Toss until the pasta is fully coated with the sauce.
16. Serve with a sprinkle of chopped basil if desired.

4.8. TAGLIATELLE

1. Tagliatelle with Bolognese Sauce

Ingredients:
- 1 pound tagliatelle pasta
- 1 tablespoon olive oil
- 1 onion, chopped
- 2 clovesgarlic, minced
- 1 poundground beef

- 1 can (14.5 ounces) crushed tomatoes
- 2 tablespoons tomato paste
- 1 teaspoon dried basil
- Salt and pepper to taste
- Grated Parmesan cheese, for serving

Instructions:
1. Fill a big saucepan with fresh water and boil on high heat.
2. Add a pinch of salt to the boiling water.
3. Gently place the homemade tagliatelle pasta in the boiling water.
4. Mix the pasta periodically to ensure it doesn't stick together.
5. Cook the pasta for about two to three minutes, or until it reaches al dente.
6. Test the pasta by biting into it. It should be tender, but still firm and not mushy. Drain and set aside.
7. In a sizable saucepan, heat the olive oil over medium temperature. Add the minced onion and sauté until it turns soft, for about five minutes.
8. Add the minced garlic and cook for another minute.
9. Pour the ground beef to the saucepan and cook until browned, breaking it apart with a wooden spoon.
10. Mix in the shredded tomatoes, salt, tomato paste, pepper and dried basil. Cook for at least ten to fifteen minutes.
11. Serve the tagliatelle pasta with the Bolognese sauce on top and sprinkle with grated Parmesan cheese.

2. Tagliatelle with Pesto Sauce

Ingredients:
- 1 pound tagliatelle pasta
- 1 cup basil leaves
- 1/2 cup grated Parmesan cheese
- 1/2 cup pine nuts

- 2 cloves garlic
- 1/2 cup olive oil
- Salt and pepper to taste
- Grated Parmesan cheese, for serving

Instructions:

1. Fill a big saucepan with fresh water and boil on high heat.
2. Add a pinch of salt to the boiling water.
3. Gently place the homemade tagliatelle pasta in the boiling water.
4. Mix the pasta periodically to ensure it doesn't stick together.
5. Cook the pasta for about two to three minutes, or until it reaches al dente.
6. Test the pasta by biting into it. It should be tender, but still firm and not mushy. Drain and set aside.
7. In a food processor or blender, mix together the pine nuts, salt basil leaves, grated Parmesan cheese, garlic, olive oil, and pepper. Blend until smooth.
8. Serve the tagliatelle pasta with the pesto sauce on top and sprinkle with grated Parmesan cheese.

4.8. TAGLIATELLE

3. Tagliatelle with Mushroom and Herb Sauce

Ingredients:

- 1 pound fresh or dried tagliatelle pasta
- 2 tablespoons unsalted butter
- 2 clovesgarlic, minced
- 8 ouncesmixed mushrooms, sliced
- 1/2 cup dry white wine
- 1/2 cup heavy cream
- 2 tablespoons chopped fresh basil
- 2 tablespoons chopped fresh thyme
- Salt and pepper to taste
- 1/4 cup grated Parmesan cheese, for serving

Instructions:

1. Fill a big saucepan with fresh water and boil.
2. Add a pinch of salt to the boiling water.
3. Gently place the homemade tagliatelle pasta in the boiling water.
4. Mix the pasta periodically to ensure it doesn't stick together.
5. Cook the pasta for about two to three minutes, or until it reaches al dente.
6. Test the pasta by biting into it. It should be tender, but still firm and not mushy. Reserve one cup of pasta water.
7. In a sizable sauté pan, warm the butter over moderate heat. Add the chopped garlic and sauté until it is fragrant, for approximately one minute.
8. Add the sliced mushrooms to the pan and cook until they are tender, and any liquid has evaporated, about five minutes.
9. Pour in the white wine and simmer until it reduces to half.
10. Stir in the heavy cream and heat until the sauce thickens slightly, approximately two to three minutes.
11. Stir in the chopped basil and thyme until well combined.
12. Season the sauce with salt and pepper to taste.
13. Drain the cooked tagliatelle pasta and add it to the pan with the mushroom and herb sauce. Toss until well combined.
14. If the sauce is too thick, loosen it with some of the remaining pasta water.
15. Serve the tagliatelle with mushroom and herb sauce, sprinkled with grated Parmesan cheese.

4. Tagliatelle with Chicken and Broccoli

Ingredients:
- 1 pound fresh tagliatelle pasta
- 1 head of broccoli, chopped
- 2 chicken breasts, diced
- 4 cloves of garlic, minced
- 1 onion, diced
- 1 cup chicken broth
- 1 cup heavy cream
- 1 cup grated Parmesan cheese
- Salt and pepper, to taste
- Olive oil, for cooking
- Fresh parsley, chopped (optional)

Instructions:
1. Fill a big saucepan with fresh water and boil.
2. Add a pinch of salt to the boiling water.
3. Gently place the homemade tagliatelle pasta in the boiling water.
4. Mix the pasta periodically to ensure it doesn't stick together.
5. Cook the pasta for about two to three minutes, or until it reaches al dente.
6. Test the pasta by biting into it. It should be tender, but still firm and not mushy. Drain and set aside.
7. In a large pan, heat some olive oil over medium heat. Add the diced onion and cook until soft and translucent, about three to four minutes.
8. Add the chopped garlic and sauté for about a minute.
9. Add the diced chicken to the pan and prepare until completely browned on every side, approximately five to seven minutes.
10. Add the sliced broccoli to the pan and cook for two to three minutes until tender.
11. Add the chicken stock and cream, and bring the mixture to a simmer.
12. Reduce the cooker to lowheat and add the grated Parmesan cheese, stirring until fully combined and the sauce has thickened.
13. Sprinkle the sauce with pepper and salt to taste.
14. Dish the cooked tagliatelle pasta in bowls and top with the chicken and broccoli sauce.
15. Garnish with freshly chopped parsley, if desired, and serve.

4.8. TAGLIATELLE

5. Tagliatelle with Shrimp and Lobster Sauce

Ingredients:

- 1 pound fresh or dried tagliatelle pasta
- 1 poundlarge shrimp, peeled and deveined
- 1/2 pound cooked lobster meat, diced
- 4 clovesgarlic, minced
- 1/2 cup white wine

- 2 tablespoons unsalted butter
- 1/2 cup heavy cream
- 1/4 cup grated Parmesan cheese
- Salt and pepper to taste
- 2 tablespoons chopped fresh parsley, for garnish

Instructions:

1. Fill a big saucepan with fresh water and boil.
2. Add a pinch of salt to the boiling water.
3. Gently place the homemade tagliatelle pasta in the boiling water.
4. Mix the pasta periodically to ensure it doesn't stick together.
5. Cook the pasta for about two to three minutes, or until it reaches al dente.
6. Test the pasta by biting into it. It should be tender, but still firm and not mushy. Reserve one cup of pasta water.
7. In a sizable sauté pan, warm the butter over moderate heat. Add the chopped garlic and sauté until it is fragrant, for approximately one minute.
8. Add the shrimp to the pan and cook until they are pink and just cooked through, about three minutes.
9. Add the diced lobster meat to the pan and cook for an additional two minutes.
10. Pour in the white wine and simmer until it reduces to half.
11. Stir in the heavy cream and heat until the sauce thickens slightly, approximately two to three minutes.
12. Stir in the grated Parmesan cheese until well combined.
13. Season the sauce with salt and pepper to taste.
14. Drain the cooked tagliatelle pasta and add it to the pan with the shrimp and lobster sauce. Toss until well combined.
15. If the sauce is too thick, loosen it with some of the remaining pasta water.
16. Serve the tagliatelle with shrimp and lobster sauce, garnished with chopped fresh parsley.

4.9. UDON

1. Udon Noodle Soup

Ingredients:

- 8 ounces dried udon noodles
- 8 cups chicken or vegetable broth
- 1 tablespoon soy sauce
- 1 tablespoon sake or rice wine
- 1 teaspoon sugar
- 1 inch fresh ginger, grated
- 2 cloves garlic, minced
- 2 green onions, sliced

- 1 carrot, thinly sliced
- 2 shiitake mushrooms, sliced
- 1 cup sliced bok choy
- 2 ouncessliced beef (optional)
- 1 egg, lightly beaten
- In two tablespoons water mix 2 tablespoons cornstarch
- 2 tablespoons sesame oil
- 1 teaspoon toasted sesame seeds

Instructions:

1. Soak the udon noodles in hot water for fifteen minutes, or until they are soft and pliable.
2. In a sizable saucepan, over high temperatures, boil the broth. Add the soy sauce, sake or rice wine, sugar, ginger, garlic, green onions, carrot, shiitake mushrooms, bok choy, and optional beef. Reduce heat to medium and let the soup simmer for ten minutes.
3. Add the beaten egg to the soup and let it cook for a minute.
4. Gradually add the cornstarch mixture to the soup, stirring constantly, until it thickens.
5. In a separate pan, heat the sesame oil over medium heat. Add the udon noodles and stir-fry them for two to three minutes, or until they are heated through.
6. Serve the udon noodles in bowls, ladle the hot soup over them, and garnish with toasted sesame seeds.

2. Udon with Shrimp

Ingredients:

- 8 ounces dried udon noodles
- 2 tablespoons vegetable oil
- 1 medium onion, chopped
- 2 clovesgarlic, minced
- 1 pound large shrimp, peeled and deveined

- 2 tablespoons soy sauce
- 2 tablespoons oyster sauce
- 1 teaspoon sugar
- 2 tablespoons water
- 1 teaspoon cornstarch
- 2 green onions, sliced for garnish

Instructions:

1. Fill a big saucepan with fresh water and boil.
2. As soon as the water begins to boil, put the udon noodles in the pot.
3. Cook the udon noodles for about eight to ten minutes, or until they are al dente.
4. To test for doneness, take out a strand of udon noodle and taste it. It should be firm but tender, with no raw flour taste.
5. Once the udon noodles are cooked, use a colander to drain and rinse them with very cold water in order to halt the cooking procedure.
6. Drain and set aside.
7. Heat the oil over medium heat in a big skillet or frying pan over medium temperature.
8. Cook until the garlic and onion are crisp, about two minutes.
9. Put the shrimp and prepare until they completely turn pink, about three to five minutes.
10. Stir in the cooked udon noodles, soy sauce, oyster sauce, and sugar.
11. In a small dish, stir together the cornstarch and water.
12. Put the cornstarch combination into the pot and stir to combine.
13. Cook for another two minutes, or until the sauce has thickened.
14. Serve hot, garnished with green onions.

4.9. UDON

3. Udon with Chicken

Ingredients:
- 8 ounces fresh udon noodles
- 1 tablespoon vegetable oil
- 1 small onion, chopped
- 2 clovesgarlic, minced
- 1 pound skinless, boneless chicken breast, chopped into tiny strips
- 2 tablespoons soy sauce

- 2 cups mixed vegetables (such as sliced carrots, bell peppers, and mushrooms)
- 1 tablespoon oyster sauce
- 1 teaspoon sugar
- In one tablespoon water mix 1 tablespoon cornstarch
- Green onions, chopped for garnish

Instructions:
1. Cook the udon noodles in boiling water for about two to three minutes or until al dente. Drain and rinse with cold water. Set aside.
2. In a sizable skillet or frying pan, heat the oil over high heat. Add the onion and garlic and stir-fry for one to two minutes.
3. Add the chicken strips and stir-fry until they are no longer pink, about four to five minutes.
4. Add the mixed vegetables and continue to stir-fry for another two to three minutes.
5. In a tiny dish, stir together the sugar, oyster sauce, cornstarch mixture, and soy sauce.
6. Layer the sauce on top of the chicken and veggies and stir for one to two minutes, or till the sauce becomes thick..
7. Serve the udon noodles topped with the chicken and vegetable mixture and garnish with chopped green onions.

4. Udon with Vegetables

Ingredients:
- 8 ounces dried udon noodles
- 2 tablespoons vegetable oil
- 1 medium onion, chopped
- 2 clovesgarlic, minced
- 2 carrots, sliced
- 2 bell peppers, sliced

- 2 cups sliced mushrooms
- 2 cups baby spinach
- 2 tablespoons soy sauce
- 2 tablespoons oyster sauce
- 1 teaspoon sugar
- 2 tablespoons water
- 1 teaspoon cornstarch

Instructions:

1. Fill a big saucepan with fresh water and boil.
2. As soon as the water begins to boil, put the udon noodles in the pot.
3. Cook the udon noodles for about eight to ten minutes, or until they are al dente.
4. To test for doneness, take out a strand of udon noodle and taste it. It should be firm but tender, with no raw flour taste.
5. Once the udon noodles are cooked, use a colander to drain and rinse them with very cold water in order to halt the cooking procedure.
6. Drain and set aside.
7. Heat the oil over medium heat in a big skillet or frying pan over medium temperature.
8. Cook until the garlic and onion are crisp, about two minutes.
9. Add the carrots, bell peppers, and mushrooms and cook for five minutes, or until the vegetables are slightly tender.
10. Stir in the cooked udon noodles, baby spinach, soy sauce, oyster sauce, and sugar.
11. In a small dish, stir together the cornstarch and water.
12. Put the cornstarch combination into the pot and stir to combine.
13. Cook for another two minutes, or until the sauce has thickened.
14. Serve hot.

4.9. UDON

5. Udon Stir-Fry

Ingredients:

- 8 ounces dried udon noodles
- 1 tablespoon vegetable oil
- 2 clovesgarlic, minced
- 1 inch fresh ginger, grated
- 1 red bell pepper, sliced
- 1 cup sliced mushrooms
- 1 cup sliced carrots
- 1 cup sliced snow peas
- 1 cup sliced bok choy
- 1 cup sliced shiitake mushrooms
- 1 cup diced chicken or shrimp (optional)
- 2 tablespoons oyster sauce
- 1 tablespoon soy sauce
- In two tablespoons water mix 2 tablespoons cornstarch
- 2 green onions, sliced

Instructions:

1. Soak the udon noodles in hot water for fifteen minutes, or until they are soft and pliable.
2. In a sizable sauté pan, heat the oil over medium-high temperatures. Add the chopped ginger and garlic and stir while frying for about thirty seconds.
3. Add the red bell pepper, mushrooms, carrots, snow peas, bok choy, shiitake mushrooms, and optional chicken or shrimp. Stir for two to three minutes maximum or until the veggies are tender and the chicken or shrimp is cooked through.
4. In a small bowl, mix together the oyster sauce, soy sauce, and cornstarch mixture.
5. Add the udon noodles to the wok or pan and stir-fry for two to three minutes, or until they are heated through.
6. Pour the sauce over the stir-fry and continue to stir-fry for another two minutes, or until the sauce has thickened.
7. Garnish with sliced green onions and serve.

4.10. SOBA

1. Soba with Vegetables

Ingredients:

- 8 ounces soba noodles
- 2 tablespoons oil
- 1 onion, sliced
- 3 clovesgarlic, minced
- 2 carrots, sliced
- 1 red bell pepper, sliced

- 2 cups sliced mushrooms
- 2 cups sliced bok choy
- 3 tablespoons soy sauce
- 2 tablespoons oyster sauce
- 2 tablespoons hoisin sauce
- 1 teaspoon sugar
- 2 green onions, chopped

Instructions:

1. Bring a sizable wok of water that has been salted to a simmer over high temperature Add the soba noodles to the boiling water, stirring gently to separate them.
2. Cook the soba noodles for about four to five minutes, or until they are tender but still firm.
3. Taste the noodles to test for doneness. They should be cooked but still have a slight bite.
4. In a colander, drain and rinse the soba noodles with cold water to halt the cooking procedure and remove amy excess starch. Drain and set aside.
5. In a sizable wok or saucepan, heat the oil over medium heat.
6. Add the onion, garlic, carrots, and red bell pepper and cook for two to three minutes until slightly softened.
7. Add the mushrooms and bok choy and cook for an additional two to three minutes.
8. Add the soy sauce, oyster sauce, hoisin sauce, and sugar to the pan and stir to combine.
9. Add the cooked soba noodles to the pan and stir to mix well with the sauce and vegetables.
10. Serve the soba noodles with vegetables hot and garnished with green onions.

2. Soba Noodle Soup

Ingredients:

- 8 ounces dried soba noodles
- 4 cups chicken or vegetable broth
- 2 cups water
- 1 tablespoon soy sauce
- 1 tablespoon sake or rice wine

- 1 teaspoon mirin
- 1 teaspoon grated ginger
- 2 clovesgarlic, minced
- 1 tablespoon green onions, sliced
- 3 ouncessliced mushrooms
- 3 ouncesdiced carrots

- 3 ounces diced bok choy
- 2 ouncessliced cooked chicken (optional)
- 1 teaspoon sesame oil
- Salt and pepper, to taste

Instructions:

1. Bring a sizable wok of water that has been salted to a simmer over high temperature.
2. Add the soba noodles to the boiling water, stir gently to separate them.
3. Cook the soba noodles for about four to five minutes, or until they are tender but still firm.
4. Taste the noodles to test for doneness. They should be cooked but still have a slight bite.
5. In a colander, drain and rinse the soba noodles with cold water to halt the cooking procedure and remove amy excess starch.
6. In a large pot, heat the chicken or vegetable broth and water over medium heat. Add the soy sauce, sake or rice wine, mirin, grated ginger, and minced garlic. Stir to combine.
7. Add the sliced mushrooms, diced carrots, and bok choy to the pot. Cook until the vegetables are soft, about five to seven minutes.
8. If desired, add the sliced cooked chicken to the pot and stir to combine.
9. In a small pan, heat the sesame oil over low heat. Add the sliced green onions and cook until fragrant, about one to two minutes.
10. Divide the cooked soba noodles into serving bowls. Pour the broth and veggies over the noodles and serve.
11. Top with the sesame oil and green onions. Season with salt and pepper, to taste.

4.10. SOBA

3. Soba with Shrimp

Ingredients:
- 8 ounces soba noodles
- 2 tablespoons oil
- 1 pound raw shrimp, peeled and deveined
- 2 clovesgarlic, minced
- 2 green onions, chopped

- 3 tablespoons soy sauce
- 2 tablespoons oyster sauce
- 2 tablespoons hoisin sauce
- 1 teaspoon sugar
- 2 tablespoons sesame oil
- Sesame seeds, for garnish

Instructions:
1. Bring a sizable wok of water that has been salted to a simmer over high temperature.
2. Add the soba noodles to the boiling water, stirring gently to separate them.
3. Cook the soba noodles for about four to five minutes, or until they are tender but still firm.
4. Taste the noodles to test for doneness. They should be cooked but still have a slight bite.
5. In a colander, drain and rinse the soba noodles with cold water to halt the cooking procedure and remove amy excess starch. Drain and set aside.
6. In a sizable wok or saucepan, heat the oil over medium heat.
7. Add the shrimp and sauté for about two to three minutes until pink and cooked through.
8. Add the garlic and green onions to the pan and cook for an additional minute.
9. Add the soy sauce, oyster sauce, hoisin sauce, and sugar to the pan and stir to combine.
10. Add the cooked soba noodles to the pan and stir to mix well with the sauce and shrimp.
11. Drizzle sesame oil over the soba noodles and shrimp and sprinkle with sesame seeds.
12. Serve the soba noodles with shrimp hot.

4. Soba Stir-Fry

Ingredients:
- 8 ounces soba noodles
- 1 tablespoon vegetable oil
- 1/2 onion, thinly sliced
- 2 clovesgarlic, minced
- 1 red bell pepper, sliced
- 1 cup sliced mushrooms
- 1 cup diced carrots

- 1 cup diced snow peas
- 1 pound chicken breast, sliced into thin strips (optional)
- 2 tablespoons soy sauce
- 1 tablespoon honey
- 1 teaspoon cornstarch
- 2 tablespoons water
- Sesame seeds for garnish (optional)

Instructions:

1. Bring a sizable wok of water that has been salted to a simmer over high temperature.
2. Add the soba noodles to the boiling water, stirring gently to separate them.
3. Cook the soba noodles for about four to five minutes, or until they are tender but still firm.
4. Taste the noodles to test for doneness. They should be cooked but still have a slight bite.
5. In a colander, drain and rinse the soba noodles with cold water to halt the cooking procedure and remove amy excess starch. Set aside.
6. In a large wok or skillet, heat the vegetable oil over high heat.
7. Add the onion, garlic, red bell pepper, mushrooms, carrots, and snow peas. Stir while frying for about two to three minutes maximum or until the veggies are tender.
8. If using chicken, add the sliced chicken to the pan and stir-fry until cooked through, about three to four minutes.
9. In a tiny dish, put together the water, soy sauce, cornstarch, and honey.
10. Add the cooked soba noodles to the pan with the vegetables and chicken. Toss to combine.
11. Layer the soy sauce combination over the soba noodles and stir to coat. Cook for an additional one to two minutes until the sauce has thickened.
12. Serve hot and garnish with sesame seeds, if desired. Enjoy!

4.10. SOBA

5. Soba with Chicken

Ingredients:
- 8 ounces soba noodles
- 1 pound skinless, boneless, chicken breasts, sliced into tiny strips
- 2 tablespoons vegetable oil
- 1/2 teaspoon salt
- 1/4 teaspoon black pepper
- 2 cloves garlic, minced
- 2 tablespoons soy sauce
- 2 cups sliced vegetables of your choice (such as bell peppers, carrots, and mushrooms)
- 1 tablespoon hoisin sauce
- 1 tablespoon rice vinegar
- 1 teaspoon sesame oil
- Sesame seeds, for garnish (optional)
- Scallions, chopped, for garnish (optional)

Instructions:
1. Bring a sizable wok of water that has been salted to a simmer over high temperature.
2. Add the soba noodles to the boiling water, stirring gently to separate them.
3. Cook the soba noodles for about four to five minutes, or until they are tender but still firm.
4. Taste the noodles to test for doneness. They should be cooked but still have a slight bite.
5. In a colander, drain and rinse the soba noodles with cold water to halt the cooking procedure and remove any excess starch. Drain and set aside.
6. In a sizable sauté pan, warm the chosen oil over medium-high heat. Add the chicken strips, salt, and pepper, and cook until browned, about three to four minutes.
7. Add the garlic and vegetables to the pan and prepare for two to three minutes, or until the vegetables are tender.
8. In a tiny dish, put together the rice vinegar, soy sauce, sesame oil, and hoisin sauce. Layer the sauce mixture over the veggies and chicken in the pan and stir to combine.
9. Add the cooked soba noodles to the pan and toss to coat with the sauce.
10. Serve the soba with chicken and vegetables hot, garnished with sesame seeds and scallions if desired.
11. Enjoy your delicious and healthy Soba with Chicken dish!

4.11. FARFALLE

1. Farfalle with Bolognese Sauce

Ingredients:

- 1 pound farfalle pasta
- 1 pound ground beef
- 1 onion, diced
- 2 clovesgarlic, minced
- 1 can (14.5 ounces) crushed tomatoes
- 2 tablespoons tomato paste
- 1/2 teaspoon dried basil
- 1/2 teaspoon dried oregano
- Salt and pepper, to taste
- 1/2 cup grated Parmesan cheese
- Fresh parsley, chopped (optional, for garnish)

Instructions:

1. Fill a sizable saucepan with fresh water filled with salt, enough to cover the pasta by at least two inches.
2. Boil the fresh water over high temperature.
3. Add the farfalle pasta to the boiling water. Mix the pasta periodically to ensure it doesn't stick together.
4. Cook the farfalle pasta for seven to eight minutes, or until it reaches your desired level of firmness. A general rule of thumb is to prepare the pasta until it is al dente, or still slightly firm when bitten.
5. In a colander, drain and rinse the soba noodles with cold water to halt the cooking procedure and set aside.
6. In a sizable pan over moderate heat, prepare the ground beef until browned, breaking it up with a wooden spoon. Drain the excess fat.
7. Add the onion and garlic to the same skillet and cook until softened, about three to five minutes.
8. Add the crushed tomatoes, tomato paste, dried basil, dried oregano, salt, and pepper. Stir to combine.
9. Turn down the temperature to low heat and allow the sauce to cook for fifteen to twenty minutes, or until it thickens.
10. Add the prepared pasta to the Bolognese sauce and mix well. Serve hot, topped with grated Parmesan cheese and fresh parsley, if desired.

2. Farfalle with Chicken and Broccoli

Ingredients:
- 8 ounces farfalle pasta
- 1 tablespoon olive oil
- 1 pound skinless, boneless, chicken breasts, sliced into bite-sized pieces
- 1/2 teaspoon salt
- 1/4 teaspoon black pepper
- 3 cloves garlic, minced
- 2 cups broccoli florets
- 1/2 cup chicken broth
- 1/4 cup heavy cream
- 1/2 cup grated Parmesan cheese

Instructions:
1. Fill a sizable saucepan with fresh water filled with salt, enough to cover the pasta by at least two inches.
2. Boil the fresh water over high temperature.
3. Add the farfalle pasta to the boiling water. Mix the pasta periodically to ensure it doesn't stick together.
4. Cook the farfalle pasta for seven to eight minutes, or until it reaches your desired level of firmness. A general rule of thumb is to prepare the pasta until it is al dente, or still slightly firm when bitten.
5. Reserve one cup of pasta water. Drain the pasta and set it to the side.
6. In a sizable skillet, warm the olive oil over moderate heat. Season the chicken pieces with salt and black pepper, then add to the skillet. Cook for five to seven minutes, until browned on all sides. Take the chicken out from the saucepan and set it to the side.
7. Add the minced garlic and broccoli florets to the skillet. Cook for three to five minutes, until the broccoli is tender.
8. Add the chicken stock as well as the heavy cream to the pot. Cook for two to three minutes, until the sauce begins to thicken.
9. Stir in the grated Parmesan cheese. Put the chicken back into the pot and toss to coat with the sauce.
10. Add the cooked farfalle pasta to the skillet and toss to combine with the chicken and sauce. In case the sauce is very thick, moisten with the reserved water from the pasta to loosen it up
11. Serve the farfalle with chicken and broccoli immediately, topped with extra Parmesan cheese and black pepper.

4.11. FARFALLE

3. Farfalle with Tomato and Basil Sauce

Ingredients:
- 8 ounces farfalle pasta
- 1 tablespoon olive oil
- 4 clovesgarlic, minced
- 2 cups cherry tomatoes, halved
- 1/2 teaspoon salt

- 1/4 teaspoon black pepper
- 1/4 teaspoon red pepper flakes (optional)
- 1/4 cup chopped fresh basil
- 1/2 cup grated Parmesan cheese
- 1/4 cup heavy cream

Instructions:

1. Fill a sizable saucepan with fresh water filled with salt, enough to cover the pasta by at least two inches.
2. Boil the fresh water over high temperature.
3. Add the farfalle pasta to the boiling water. Mix the pasta periodically to ensure it doesn't stick together.
4. Cook the farfalle pasta for seven to eight minutes, or until it reaches your desired level of firmness. A general rule of thumb is to prepare the pasta until it is al dente, or still slightly firm when bitten.
5. Reserve one cup of pasta water. Drain the pasta and keep by the side.
6. In a sizable skillet, warm the olive oil over moderate heat. Add the chopped garlic and simmer for about a minute, until fragrant.
7. In the saucepan, add the cherry tomatoes. Season with pepper, red pepper flakes and salt to taste (if using). Simmer, stirring periodically, for five to seven minutes, or until the tomatoes soften.
8. Stir in the chopped basil, grated Parmesan cheese, and heavy cream. Cook for two to three minutes, until the sauce begins to thicken.
9. Add the cooked farfalle pasta to the skillet and toss to coat with the basil sauce. In case the sauce is very thick, moisten with the reserved water from the pasta to loosen it up
10. Serve the farfalle with tomato and basil sauce immediately, topped with extra Parmesan cheese and fresh basil.

4. Farfalle with Shrimp Scampi

Ingredients:
- 1 pound farfalle pasta
- 1 pound large shrimp, peeled and deveined
- 1/2 cup unsalted butter
- 4 clovesgarlic, minced
- 1/2 cup dry white wine
- 1 lemon, juiced
- 1/4 cup heavy cream
- 1/4 cup chopped parsley
- Salt and pepper to taste

Instructions:
1. Cook farfalle pasta in a large pot of boiling salted water until al dente, about ten to twelve minutes. Drain and set aside.
2. In a large skillet, melt the butter over medium temperature. Add the chopped garlic and sauté till fragrant, for about a minute.
3. Add the shrimp to the saucepan and cook for two to three minutes on either side, or until pink and moderately firm. Take the shrimp out of the saucepan and set it aside.
4. In the same skillet, add the white wine and lemon juice, stirring to scrape up any browned bits from the bottom of the pan.
5. Stir in the heavy cream and bring the mixture to a simmer. Prepare til the sauce has slightly thickened, for about five minutes.
6. Return the cooked shrimp to the skillet and add the chopped parsley. Season with salt and pepper to taste.
7. Serve the shrimp scampi mixture over cooked farfalle pasta, garnishing with additional parsley if desired.

4.11. FARFALLE

5. Farfalle with Pesto Sauce

Ingredients:
- 1 pound farfalle pasta
- 1 cup basil leaves
- 1/2 cup grated Parmesan cheese
- 1/2 cup pine nuts
- 2 cloves garlic
- 1/2 cup olive oil
- Salt and pepper, to taste
- 1/2 cup reserved pasta water
- Fresh basil leaves, chopped (optional, for garnish)

Instructions:
1. Fill a sizable saucepan with fresh water filled with salt, enough to cover the pasta by at least two inches.
2. Boil the fresh water over high temperature.
3. Add the farfalle pasta to the boiling water. Mix the pasta periodically to ensure it doesn't stick together.
4. Cook the farfalle pasta for seven to eight minutes, or until it reaches your desired level of firmness. A general rule of thumb is to prepare the pasta until it is al dente, or still slightly firm when bitten.
5. In a colander, drain and rinse the soba noodles with cold water to halt the cooking procedure
6. Reserve half cup of pasta water and set both aside.
7. In a food processor, combine the basil, Parmesan cheese, pine nuts, garlic, and olive oil. Process until the mixture becomes a smooth pesto.
8. In a sizable dish, stir the pesto with the reserved pasta water until well combined.
9. Mix the prepared pasta with the pesto combinations and mix well. Serve hot, topped with fresh basil leaves, if desired.

4.12. PENNE

1. Penne alla Vodka

Ingredients:
- 1 pound penne pasta
- 1/2 cup unsalted butter
- 1 medium onion, chopped
- 2 clovesgarlic, minced
- 1 cup heavy cream
- 1/2 cup tomato sauce
- 1/4 teaspoon crushed red pepper flakes
- 1/2 cup vodka
- 1/2 cup grated Parmesan cheese
- Salt and pepper, to taste

Instructions:
1. Fill a large pot with water, add a pinch of salt, and boil.
2. Once the water is boiling, add the homemade penne pasta. Stir the pasta to prevent it from sticking together.
3. Cook the penne pasta for about eight to ten minutes or until it is al dente.
4. To test if the pasta is al dente, remove a piece of pasta from the pot and bite into it. The pasta should be cooked but still firm.
5. In a colander, drain and rinse the pasta with cold water once it is ready.
6. In a sizable pot, melt all the butter over moderate temperature.
7. Add the chopped garlic and onion to the saucepan and prepare until the onion becomes soft and completely translucent, about five minutes.
8. Stir in the heavy cream, tomato sauce, crushed red pepper flakes, and vodka.
9. Reduce to low heat and allow the sauce to cook for ten minutes, or until it has thickened slightly.
10. Stir in the Parmesan cheese until melted. Season the sauce with salt and pepper to taste.
11. Toss the cooked penne pasta with the sauce and serve hot.

2. Penne with Tomato and Basil Sauce

Ingredients:
- 1 pound penne pasta
- 2 tablespoons olive oil
- 1 large onion, chopped
- 4 clovesgarlic, minced
- 2 cans of diced tomatoes
- 2 tablespoons tomato paste
- 1/2 teaspoon sugar
- Salt and pepper, to taste
- 1 cup fresh basil leaves, chopped
- 1/2 cup grated Parmesan cheese

Instructions:

1. Fill a large pot with water, add a little bit of salt, and boil.
2. Once the water is boiling, add the homemade penne pasta. Stir the pasta to prevent it from sticking together.
3. Cook the penne pasta for about eight to ten minutes or until it is al dente.
4. To test if the pasta is al dente, remove a piece of pasta from the pot and bite into it. The pasta should be cooked but still firm.
5. In a colander, drain and rinse the pasta with cold water once it is ready.
6. In a large saucepan, heat the olive oil over medium heat.
7. Add the onion and garlic to the pan and cook until the onion is soft and translucent, about five minutes.
8. Stir in the diced tomatoes, tomato paste, and sugar. Season the sauce with salt and pepper to taste.
9. Let the sauce simmer for ten minutes, or until it has thickened slightly.
10. Stir in the basil leaves until wilted.
11. Toss the cooked penne pasta with the sauce and serve hot, topped with grated Parmesan cheese.

4.12. PENNE

3. Penne with Shrimp Scampi

Ingredients:
- 8 ounces penne pasta
- 1 pound large shrimp, peeled and deveined
- 4 garlic cloves, minced
- 1/4 cup dry white wine
- 1/4 cup chicken broth
- 2 tablespoons lemon juice
- 2 tablespoons unsalted butter
- Salt and black pepper, to taste
- 1/4 cup fresh parsley, chopped

Instructions:
1. Fill a large pot with water, add a bit of salt, and boil.
2. Once the water is boiling, add the homemade penne pasta. Stir the pasta to prevent it from sticking together.
3. Cook the penne pasta for about eight to ten minutes or until it is al dente.
4. To test if the pasta is al dente, remove a piece of pasta from the pot and bite into it. The pasta should be cooked but still firm.
5. In a colander, drain and rinse the pasta with cold water once it is ready. Reserve 1/2 cup of pasta water.
6. In a sizable pot, heat olive oil over moderate heat. Add chopped garlic and prepare until fragrant, for approximately one minute.
7. Add shrimp to the skillet and cook until pink, about two to three minutes per side.
8. Pour in the white wine, chicken broth, and lemon juice. Sauté for about two to three minutes, or till the sauce has reduced by half.
9. Remove the skillet from heat and whisk in the butter. Season the sauce with salt and black pepper, to taste.
10. In a sizable pot, put together prepared pasta with shrimp scampi sauce. Toss to evenly coat.
11. In case the pasta looks dry, moisten with a little bit of the reserved pasta water to loosen it up.
12. Serve hot and garnish with parsley, if desired.

4. Penne with Pesto Sauce

Ingredients:
- 8 ounces penne pasta
- 1 cup fresh basil leaves
- 1/2 cup freshly grated Parmesan cheese
- 1/2 cup pine nuts
- 4 garlic cloves, minced
- 1/2 cup extra-virgin olive oil
- Salt and black pepper, to taste
- 1/2 cup cherry tomatoes, halved

Instructions:
1. Fill a large pot with water, add a pinch of salt, and bring to a boil.
2. Once the water is boiling, add the homemade penne pasta. Stir the pasta to prevent it from sticking together.
3. Cook the penne pasta for about eight to ten minutes or until it is al dente.
4. To test if the pasta is al dente, remove a piece of pasta from the pot and bite into it. The pasta should be cooked but still firm.
5. In a colander, drain and rinse the pasta with cold water once it is ready. Reserve 1/2 cup of pasta water.
6. In a food processor, combine basil, Parmesan cheese, pine nuts, and garlic. Pulse until well combined.
7. With the food machine running, gently pour in the olive oil. Continue to blend until the mixture is smooth.
8. Season the pesto sauce with salt and black pepper, to taste.
9. In a sizable dish, mixed together pesto sauce with cooked pasta and cherry tomatoes. Toss to evenly coat.
10. In case the pasta looks dry, moist with a little bit of the reserved pasta water to loosen it up.
11. Serve hot and garnish with additional Parmesan cheese and basil, if desired.

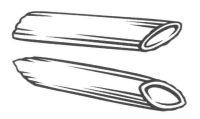

4.12. PENNE

5. Penne with Chicken and Broccoli

Ingredients:
- 1 pound penne pasta
- 2 tablespoons olive oil
- 1 medium onion, chopped
- 2 clovesarlic, minced
- 2 medium boneless, skinless chicken breasts, cut into bite-sized pieces
- 1 head of broccoli, chopped into florets

- 1/2 teaspoon dried basil
- 1/2 teaspoon dried oregano
- 1/4 teaspoon red pepper flakes (optional)
- 1 cup chicken broth
- 1/2 cup heavy cream
- 1/2 cup grated Parmesan cheese
- Salt and pepper, to taste

Instructions:
1. Fill a large pot with water, add a little bit of salt, and boil.
2. Once the water is boiling, add the homemade penne pasta. Stir the pasta to prevent it from sticking together.
3. Cook the penne pasta for about eight to ten minutes or until it is al dente.
4. To test if the pasta is al dente, remove a piece of pasta from the pot and bite into it. The pasta should be cooked but still firm.
5. In a colander, drain and rinse the pasta with cold water once it is ready.
6. In a sizable pot, warm the olive oil over medium temperature. Add the chopped onion as well as the garlic and prepare until softened, approximately five minutes.
7. Cook the chicken in the saucepan until browned, approximately five to seven minutes.
8. Add the broccoli to the skillet and cook until tender, about five minutes.
9. Stir in the basil, oregano, and red pepper flakes (if using).
10. Add in the chicken stock and the heavy cream. Stir to combine.
11. Bring the mix to a gentle boil and cook for five minutes, till the sauce has slightly thickened.
12. Mix in the shredded Parmesan cheese and sprinkle with pepper and salt to taste.
13. Dish the penne with the chicken and broccoli sauce spooned over the top. Enjoy!

4.13. RAVIOLI

1. Classic Cheese Ravioli

Ingredients:
- 1 recipe of homemade pasta dough
- 1 cup of ricotta cheese
- 1/2 cup of grated Parmesan cheese
- 1/2 cup of grated mozzarella cheese
- 1 egg
- Salt and pepper to taste

Instructions:
1. Make the pasta dough as per the recipe and roll it out into thin sheets.
2. In a dish, stir together the eggs, ricotta cheese, Parmesan cheese, mozzarella cheese, salt, and pepper.
3. Place small spoonfuls of the cheese mixture onto one of the pasta sheets, leaving about 1 1/2 inches of space between each spoonful.
4. Brush the edges of each pasta square with a bit of water and then place the other pasta sheet on top, pressing down around each spoonful of cheese mixture to seal the ravioli.
5. Cut the ravioli into squares using a sharp knife.
6. Repeat the process with the remaining pasta and cheese mixture.
7. Boil the ravioli in salted water for about three to four minutes or till they completely float to the surface.
8. Serve with your favorite sauce.

2. Spinach and Ricotta Ravioli

Ingredients:
- 1 recipe of homemade pasta dough
- 1 cup of cooked spinach, drained and chopped
- 1 cup of ricotta cheese
- 1/2 cup of grated Parmesan cheese
- 1 egg
- Salt and pepper to taste

Instructions:
1. Make the pasta dough as per the recipe and roll it out into thin sheets.
2. In a sizable dish, stir together the eggs, ricotta cheese, cooked spinach, Parmesan cheese, salt, and pepper.

3. Place small spoonfuls of the cheese and spinach mixture onto one of the pasta sheets, leaving about 1 1/2 inches of space between each spoonful.
4. Brush the edges of each pasta square with a bit of water and then place the other pasta sheet on top, pressing down around each spoonful of cheese mixture to seal the ravioli.
5. Cut the ravioli into squares using a sharp knife.
6. Repeat the process with the remaining pasta and cheese mixture.
7. Boil the ravioli in salted water for about three to four minutes or till they completely float to the surface.
8. Serve with your favorite sauce.

3. Butternut Squash Ravioli

Ingredients:
- 1 medium butternut squash
- 1 egg
- 1/2 cup grated Parmesan cheese
- Salt and pepper to taste
- Fresh pasta dough
- Flour for dusting

Instructions:
1. Preheat oven to 400 degrees Farenheit [200°C].
2. Slice the butternut squash in half and scoop out the seeds.
3. Arrange the squash halves sliced side up on a baking tray and sprinkle with olive oil.
4. Bake the squash for thirty to forty minutes, or till when it becomes tender and softened.
5. Remove from the oven and let cool.
6. In a bowl, mash the butternut squash until smooth.
7. Stir in the egg, Parmesan cheese, salt, and pepper.
8. Spread the pasta dough out on a moderately floured surface.
9. Cut the pasta into rounds, about two to three inches in diameter.
10. Spoon a small amount of the butternut squash mixture into the center of each round.
11. Brush the edges of the pasta with a bit of water and fold over to seal.
12. Repeat the process with the remaining pasta rounds and filling.
13. Boil the ravioli in salted water until they float to the surface, about two to three minutes.
14. Serve with your favorite sauce.

4.13. RAVIOLI

4. Mushroom and Herb Ravioli

Ingredients:
- 1 pound mushrooms, chopped
- 1 onion, chopped
- 4 cloves of garlic, minced.
- 1/4 cup fresh parsley, chopped
- 1/4 cup fresh basil, chopped
- Salt and pepper to taste
- Fresh pasta dough
- Flour for dusting

Instructions:
1. In a large skillet, heat a bit of oil over medium temperature.
2. Add the onion, mushrooms, and chopped garlic and cook until the mushrooms are tender, about eight to ten minutes.
3. Stir in the parsley and basil and season with salt and pepper.
4. Remove from the heat and let cool.
5. Spread the pasta dough out on a moderately floured surface.
6. Cut the pasta into rounds, about two to three inches in diameter.
7. Spoon a small amount of the mushroom mixture into the center of each round.
8. Brush the edges of the pasta with a bit of water and fold over to seal.
9. Repeat the process with the remaining pasta rounds and filling.
10. Boil the ravioli in salted water until they float to the surface, about two to three minutes.
11. Serve with your favorite sauce.

5. Shrimp and Lobster Ravioli

Ingredients:
- 1 pound of fresh or frozen shrimp, peeled and deveined
- 1 pound of fresh or frozen lobster meat, chopped
- 1 egg
- 1/2 cup of ricotta cheese
- 1/2 cup of grated Parmesan cheese
- 2 tablespoons of chopped fresh parsley
- 1 teaspoon of dried basil
- Salt and pepper, to taste
- 1 batch of pasta dough
- Egg wash (one stirred egg beaten with one tablespoon of water)

Instructions:

1. In a food processor, blend the shrimp and lobster meat until it forms a smooth paste.
2. In a large bowl, mix the shrimp and lobster paste with the egg, ricotta cheese, Parmesan cheese, parsley, basil, salt, and pepper.
3. On a moderately floured surface, spread out the pasta dough to about 1/8 inch thickness.
4. Cut the pasta dough into two-inch squares.
5. Place a small spoonful of the shrimp and lobster filling in the center of each square.
6. Brush the egg wash along the corners of the pasta cubes.
7. Fold the pasta squares in half, forming a triangle and pressing the edges to seal.
8. Cut the ravioli along the creased edges to separate them.
9. Repeat the process with the remaining pasta dough as well as filling.
10. Bring a sizable pot of salted water to a boil.
11. Cook the ravioli in the boiling water for two to three minutes or until they float to the surface.
12. Serve with your favorite sauce and garnish with grated Parmesan cheese and fresh parsley.

4.14. ORECCHIETTE

1. Orecchiette with Broccoli Rabe and Sausage

Ingredients:
- 1 pound orecchiette pasta
- 1 head of broccoli rabe, chopped
- 4 Italian sausages, casings removed
- 4 cloves of garlic, minced

- 1/4 cup extra-virgin olive oil
- 1/2 cup chicken broth
- 1/2 cup grated Pecorino Romano cheese
- Salt and black pepper, to taste

Instructions:
1. Fill a large pot with water, add a little bit of salt, and boil.
2. Once the water is boiling, add the orecchiette pasta. Stir the pasta to prevent it from sticking together.
3. Cook the orecchiette pasta for about eight to ten minutes or until it is al dente.
4. In a sizable saucepan, heat the olive oil over moderate heat.
5. Add the sausage and cook until browned, breaking it up into small pieces as it cooks.
6. Add the garlic and broccoli rabe to the pan with the sausage and cook until the broccoli rabe is wilted, about two minutes.
7. Add the chicken stock to the saucepan and bring to a boil.
8. Drain the pasta and put it in the saucepan with the sausage mixture.
9. Toss the pasta with the sausage mixture until well combined.
10. Add the grated Pecorino Romano cheese and season with salt and black pepper, to taste.
11. Serve hot and garnish with additional cheese and black pepper, if desired.

2. Orecchiette with Sun-Dried Tomatoes and Spinach

Ingredients:
- 1 pound orecchiette pasta
- 1/2 cup sun-dried tomatoes, chopped
- 4 cloves of garlic, minced
- 1/2 cup chicken broth

- 1 cup fresh spinach
- 1/2 cup grated Parmesan cheese
- Salt and black pepper, to taste
- 1/4 cup extra-virgin olive oil

Instructions:

1. Fill a large pot with water, add a little bit of salt, and boil.
2. Once the water is boiling, add the orecchiette pasta. Stir the pasta to prevent it from sticking together.
3. Cook the orecchiette pasta for about eight to ten minutes or until it is al dente.
4. In a sizable saucepan, heat the olive oil over moderate heat.
5. Add the sun-dried tomatoes and chop and sauté until fragrant, about one minute.
6. Put the chicken stock in the saucepan and bring to a boil.
7. Add the sliced spinach to the saucepan and cook until wilted, about two minutes.
8. Drain the pasta and put it in the saucepan with the tomato mixture.
9. Toss the pasta with the tomato mixture until well combined.
10. Add the shredded Parmesan cheese and sprinkle with black pepper and salt to taste.
11. Serve hot and garnish with additional cheese and black pepper, if desired.

3. Orecchiette with Broccoli and Garlic

Ingredients:

- 1 pound orecchiette pasta
- 1 broccoli head, sliced into tiny florets
- 4 garlic cloves, minced

- 1/2 cup olive oil
- 1/2 cup grated Parmesan cheese
- Salt and pepper, to taste

Instructions:

1. Fill a large pot with water, add a little bit of salt, and boil.
2. Once the water is boiling, add the orecchiette pasta. Stir the pasta to prevent it from sticking together.
3. Cook the orecchiette pasta for about eight to ten minutes or until it is al dente or firm.
4. While the pasta is cooking, heat the olive oil in a large saucepan over medium temperature.
5. Add the minced garlic to the pan and cook until fragrant, about one minute.
6. Add the chopped broccoli florets to the saucepan and cook until tender, about five minutes.
7. Reserve one cup of pasta H2O [water] or bowl and drain the orecchiette pasta in a colander.
8. Add the cooked orecchiette pasta to the pan with the broccoli and garlic. Toss to combine.
9. In case the pasta looks dry, moisten it by adding a little of the reserved pasta water to loosen it up.
10. Serve the pasta with a sprinkle of shredded Parmesan cheese and sprinkle with pepper and salt to taste

4.14. ORECCHIETTE

4. Orecchiette with Sausage and Peppers

Ingredients:

- 1 pound orecchiette pasta
- 4 Italian sausages, casings removed
- 2 red bell peppers, sliced
- 2 yellow bell peppers, sliced
- 1 onion, chopped
- 4 garlic cloves, minced
- 1/2 cup olive oil
- Salt and pepper, to taste

Instructions:

1. Fill a large pot with water, add a little bit of salt, and boil.
2. Once the water is boiling, add the orecchiette pasta. Stir the pasta to prevent it from sticking together.
3. Cook the orecchiette pasta for about eight to ten minutes or until it is al dente or firm.
4. While the pasta is cooking, heat the olive oil in a large saucepan over medium temperature.
5. Cook till the sausage is browned, dividing it up into little pieces as it heats.
6. Add the onion, bell peppers, and garlic to the pan and cook until tender, about five minutes.
7. Reserve one cup of pasta H2O [water] and drain the orecchiette pasta in a colander.
8. Add the cooked orecchiette pasta to the pan with the sausage and vegetables. Toss to combine.
9. In case the pasta looks dry, moisten by adding a little bit of the reserved pasta water to loosen it up.
10. Serve the pasta hot and season with salt and pepper, to taste.

4.15. CAPELLINI (ANGEL HAIR)

1. Garlic and Olive Oil Angel Hair Pasta

Ingredients:
- 8 ounces capellini pasta
- 1/4 cup extra-virgin olive oil
- 4 garlic cloves, minced
- Salt and black pepper, to taste
- 1/4 cup freshly grated Parmesan cheese
- 2 tablespoons chopped fresh parsley

Instructions:
1. Fill a large pot with water, add a little bit of salt, and boil.
2. Once the water is boiling, add the angel hair pasta. Stir the pasta to prevent it from sticking together.
3. Cook the angel hair pasta for about two to three minutes or until it is al dente.
4. To test if the pasta is al dente, remove a piece of pasta from the pot and bite into it. The pasta should be cooked but still firm.
5. After the pasta has finished cooking, in a colander drain and rinse in very cold water. Save 1/2 cup of pasta water.
6. Place a large saucepan over medium heat and warm the olive oil.
7. Add the chopped garlic and simmer for one to two minutes, or until fragrant.
8. Return the prepared pasta to the saucepan and mix in the olive oil and garlic.
9. Add black pepper and salt to taste.
10. To loosen the pasta if it appears to be dry, add a small amount of the pasta water that was set aside.
11. Sprinkle chopped parsley and shredded Parmesan cheese. Serve hot.

2. Lemon and Shrimp Angel Hair Pasta

Ingredients:
- 8 ounces capellini pasta
- 1 pound medium shrimp, peeled and deveined
- 1/4 cup extra-virgin olive oil
- 4 garlic cloves, minced
- 1 lemon, juiced
- Salt and black pepper, to taste
- 1/4 cup freshly grated Parmesan cheese
- 2 tablespoons chopped fresh parsley

Instructions:

1. Fill a large pot with water, add a little bit of salt, and boil.
2. Once the water is boiling, add the angel hair pasta. Stir the pasta to prevent it from sticking together.
3. Cook the angel hair pasta for about two to three minutes or until it is al dente.
4. To test if the pasta is al dente, remove a piece of pasta from the pot and bite into it. The pasta should be cooked but still firm.
5. After the pasta has finished cooking, in a colander drain and rinse in very cold water. Save 1/2 cup of pasta water.
6. Place a large saucepan over medium heat and warm the olive oil.
7. Add the chopped garlic and simmer for one to two minutes, or until fragrant.
8. Put the shrimp into the pot and prepare until pink, about two to three minutes.
9. Add the prepared pasta to the saucepan and toss with the shrimp and garlic.
10. Squeeze the lemon juice over the pasta and toss to evenly coat.
11. Sprinkle with black pepper and salt, to taste.
12. In case the pasta looks dry, add a little bit of the reserved pasta water to loosen it up.
13. Sprinkle with sliced parsley and shredded Parmesan cheese. Serve hot.

4.15. CAPELLINI (ANGEL HAIR)

3. Tomato and Basil Angel Hair Pasta

Ingredients:

- 1 pound capellini pasta (capellini)
- 1/2 cup extra-virgin olive oil
- 4 garlic cloves, minced
- 1/2 teaspoon red pepper flakes
- 2 pints cherry tomatoes, halved
- 1/2 cup fresh basil leaves, chopped
- Salt and black pepper, to taste
- 1/2 cup freshly grated Parmesan cheese

Instructions:

1. Fill a large pot with water, add a little bit of salt, and boil.
2. Once the water is boiling, add the angel hair pasta. Stir the pasta to prevent it from sticking together.
3. Cook the pasta for about two to three minutes or until it is al dente.
4. To test if the pasta is al dente, remove a piece of pasta from the pot and bite into it. The pasta should be cooked but still firm.
5. After the pasta has finished cooking, in a colander drain and rinse in very cold water. Save 1/2 cup of pasta water.
6. Place a large saucepan over medium heat and warm the olive oil. Add the chopped garlic and sliced red pepper flakes and prepare until fragrant, about one minute.
7. Add the soft cherry tomatoes and sauté until they begin to soften, about four to five minutes.
8. Stir in the chopped basil and season with salt and black pepper, to taste.
9. In a sizable bowl, put together prepared pasta with the tomato basil sauce. Toss to evenly coat.
10. In case the pasta looks dry, moisten with a little bit of the reserved pasta water to loosen it up.
11. Serve hot and garnish with additional Parmesan cheese and basil, if desired.

4.16. FUSILLI (SPIRAL)

1. Fusilli with Pesto and Cherry Tomatoes

Ingredients:
- 1 pound fusilli pasta
- 1/2 cup basil pesto
- 1 pint cherry tomatoes, halved
- 1/4 cup grated Parmesan cheese
- Salt and black pepper, to taste

Instructions:
1. Fill a large pot with water, add a little bit of salt, and boil.
2. Once the water is boiling, add the fusilli pasta. Stir the pasta to prevent it from sticking together.
3. Cook the fusilli pasta for about eight to ten minutes or until it is al dente.
4. To test if the pasta is al dente, remove a piece of pasta from the pot and bite into it. The pasta should be cooked but still firm.
5. After the pasta has finished cooking, in a colander drain and rinse in very cold water. Save 1/2 cup of pasta water.
6. In a sizable bowl, put together the prepared pasta with basil pesto, cherry tomatoes, and grated Parmesan cheese. Toss to evenly coat.
7. In case the pasta looks dry, moisten with a little bit of the reserved pasta water to loosen it up.
8. Sprinkle with black pepper and salt, to taste.
9. Divide hot and garnish with additional Parmesan cheese and basil, if desired.

2. Fusilli with Spicy Tomato Sauce

Ingredients:
- 1 pound fusilli pasta
- 1 tablespoon olive oil
- 1 medium onion, finely chopped
- 3 garlic cloves, minced
- 1 teaspoon dried red pepper flakes
- 1 can (14.5 ounces) of diced tomatoes
- 1/2 teaspoon sugar
- Salt and pepper, to taste
- 1/4 cup fresh basil leaves, chopped
- Grated Parmesan cheese, for serving

Instructions:

1. Fill a large pot with water, add a little bit of salt, and boil.
2. Once the water is boiling, add the fusilli pasta. Stir the pasta to prevent it from sticking together.
3. Cook the fusilli pasta for about eight to ten minutes or until it is al dente.
4. Reserve 1/2 cup of pasta water.
5. Place a large saucepan over medium heat and warm the olive oil.
6. Add the chopped garlic, onion, and dried red pepper flakes. Prepare till the onion is completely soft, for approximately five minutes.
7. Stir in the canned tomatoes and sugar. Season with salt and pepper to taste.
8. Simmer the sauce for about ten minutes, until it has thickened slightly.
9. Add the fresh basil to the sauce and stir to combine.
10. In a sizable bowl, put together the prepared pasta and tomato sauce. Toss to evenly coat.
11. In case the pasta looks dry, moisten with a little bit of the reserved pasta water to loosen it up.
12. Serve the fusilli with spicy tomato sauce and grated Parmesan cheese on top. Enjoy!

4.16. FUSILLI (SPIRAL)

3. Fusilli with Broccoli Rabe and Sausage

Ingredients:
- 1 pound fusilli pasta
- 1 bunch of broccoli rabe, trimmed and chopped
- 4 Italian sausages, casings removed
- 4 garlic cloves, minced
- 1/4 cup olive oil
- Salt and black pepper, to taste

Instructions:
1. Fill a large pot with water, add a little bit of salt, and boil.
2. Once the water is boiling, add the fusilli pasta. Stir the pasta to prevent it from sticking together.
3. Cook the fusilli pasta for about eight to ten minutes or until it is al dente.
4. To test if the pasta is al dente, remove a piece of pasta from the pot and bite into it. The pasta should be cooked but still firm.
5. After the pasta has finished cooking, in a colander drain and rinse in very cold water. Save 1/2 cup of pasta water.
6. Place a large saucepan over medium heat and warm the olive oil. Add chopped garlic and cook for approximately one minute or until fragrant.
7. Add in the sausage and cook, breaking it into small pieces, until browned and crispy, about five minutes.
8. Add the chopped broccoli rabe to the wok and cook until it is wilted, about three to five minutes.
9. In a large bowl, combine cooked pasta, sausage and broccoli rabe mixture, and reserved pasta water. Toss to evenly coat.
10. Sprinkle with black pepper and salt, to taste.
11. Serve hot and garnish with grated Parmesan cheese, if desired.

4. Creamy Tomato and Spinach Fusilli

Ingredients:
- 1 pound fusilli pasta
- 2 tablespoons olive oil
- 1 small onion, chopped
- 3 garlic cloves, minced
- 1 can (14.5 ounces) diced tomatoes

- 1/2 cup heavy cream
- 1/2 teaspoon red pepper flakes
- 1/2 teaspoon salt
- 1/4 teaspoon black pepper

- 2 cups baby spinach, chopped
- 1/4 cup grated Parmesan cheese
- Fresh basil leaves for garnish

Instructions:

1. Fill a large pot with water, add a little bit of salt, and boil.
2. Once the water is boiling, add the fusilli pasta. Stir the pasta to prevent it from sticking together.
3. Cook the fusilli pasta for about eight to ten minutes or until it is firm or al dente. Set aside after draining.
4. Place a large saucepan over medium heat and warm the olive oil. Add the onion and garlic and sauté until the onion is translucent, about five minutes.
5. Add the diced tomatoes, red pepper flakes, salt, and black pepper to the skillet. Cook for five to ten minutes or until the sauce thickens.
6. Stir in the heavy cream and chopped spinach, cooking until the spinach has wilted and the sauce has thickened.
7. Add the cooked fusilli to the skillet and toss\shake to coat the fusilli pasta with the sauce.
8. Sprinkle the grated Parmesan cheese over the top of the pasta and stir to combine.
9. Serve immediately, garnished with fresh basil leaves. Enjoy!

4.17. RADIATORI (RADIATOR-LIKE)

1. Radiatori with Pesto and Roasted Vegetables

Ingredients:
- 1 pound radiatori pasta
- 2 zucchini, chopped
- 2 bell peppers, chopped
- 1 red onion, chopped
- 3 garlic cloves, minced
- 1/4 cup extra-virgin olive oil
- Salt and black pepper, to taste
- 1 cup basil pesto
- 1/2 cup grated Parmesan cheese

Instructions:
1. Preheat the oven to 425°F.
2. On a sizable baking sheet, shake\toss together the zucchini, bell peppers, red onion, garlic, olive oil, salt, and black pepper. Roast for twenty to twenty-five minutes or until vegetables are tender and slightly charred.
3. Fill a large pot with water, add a little bit of salt, and boil.
4. Once the water is boiling, add the radiatori pasta. Stir the pasta to prevent it from sticking together.
5. Cook the radiatori pasta for about eight to ten minutes or until it is al dente.
6. To test if the pasta is al dente, remove a piece of pasta from the pot and bite into it. The pasta should be cooked but still firm.
7. After the pasta has finished cooking, in a colander drain and rinse in very cold water.
8. In a sizable bowl, put together the prepared pasta, roasted vegetables, basil pesto, and Parmesan cheese. Toss to evenly coat.
9. Serve hot and garnish with additional Parmesan cheese and basil, if desired.

2. Radiatori with Tomato and Basil Sauce

Ingredients:
- 1 pound radiatori pasta
- 1 tablespoon olive oil
- 2 garlic cloves, minced
- 28 ounce of crushed tomatoes
- 1/2 teaspoon salt
- 1/4 teaspoon black pepper
- 1/4 teaspoon red pepper flakes
- 1/4 cup fresh basil leaves, chopped
- Grated Parmesan cheese for serving

Instructions:

1. Fill a large pot with water, add a little bit of salt, and boil.
2. Once the water is boiling, add the radiatori pasta. Stir the pasta to prevent it from sticking together.
3. Cook the radiatori pasta for about eight to ten minutes or until it is al dente.
4. While the radiatori pasta is cooking, heat the olive oil in a large saucepan over moderate heat.
5. Add the chopped garlic and sauté for approximately one to two minutes or until fragrant.
6. Add the crushed tomatoes, salt, black pepper, and red pepper flakes. Mix everything together and bring the uncooked sauce to a boil.
7. Simmer the sauce for ten to fifteen minutes, stirring now and then, or until it slightly thickens.
8. When the pasta is done cooking, reserve half a cup of the radiatori pasta H2O [water] and then drain the entire pasta.
9. Add the cooked radiatori to the saucepan with the tomato sauce, along with the reserved pasta water.
10. Toss\shake the pasta with the prepared sauce to coat, then add the chopped basil and toss again.
11. Serve the radiatori hot with grated Parmesan cheese on top. Enjoy!

4.17. RADIATORI (RADIATOR-LIKE)

3. Radiatori with Creamy Shrimp Scampi Sauce

Ingredients:

- 8 ounces radiatori pasta
- 1 pound large shrimp, peeled and deveined
- 4 tablespoons butter
- 4 cloves of garlic, minced
- 1/2 cup white wine
- 1/2 cup heavy cream
- 1/2 cup grated Parmesan cheese
- 1/4 teaspoon red pepper flakes
- 1 lemon, juiced
- Salt and pepper, to taste
- 2 tablespoons chopped parsley, for garnish

Instructions:

1. Fill a sizable saucepan with salted H2O [water] and boil. Add the radiatori pasta and cook for about eight to ten minutes or until al dente.
2. While the pasta is cooking, in a large saucepan over medium temperature, melt two tablespoons of butter.
3. Put the shrimp in the pot and prepare until pink, about two to three minutes. Take the shrimp out of the skillet and place them aside.
4. In the same pot, put in the remaining two tablespoons of butter and the minced garlic. Cook until fragrant, about one minute.
5. Add the white wine to the skillet and bring to a boil. Let the wine reduce by half.
6. Stir in the heavy cream, Parmesan cheese, red pepper flakes, lemon juice, salt, and pepper.
7. Reduce to low heat and allow the sauce cook for about to three minutes or until slightly thickened.
8. Add the prepared shrimp back to the pot and let the sauce heat through.
9. Drain the cooked radiatori pasta and add it to the skillet with the shrimp and scampi sauce. Toss to coat.
10. Serve the radiatori with a sprinkle of shredded Parmesan cheese and additional chopped parsley, if desired. Enjoy!

4. Radiatori Carbonara

Ingredients:
- 1 pound radiatori pasta
- 8 ounces bacon, chopped
- 1/2 cup grated Parmesan cheese
- 2 large eggs
- 2 egg yolks
- Salt and black pepper, to taste
- 1/4 cup chopped parsley

Instructions:
1. Fill a large pot with water, add a little bit of salt, and boil
2. Once the water is boiling, add the radiatori pasta. Stir the pasta to prevent it from sticking together.
3. Cook the radiatori pasta for about eight to ten minutes or until it is al dente.
4. To test if the pasta is al dente, remove a piece of pasta from the pot and bite into it. The pasta should be cooked but still firm.
5. After the pasta has finished cooking, in a colander drain and rinse in very cold water. Save 1/2 cup of pasta water.
6. In a sizable saucepan, prepare the bacon over moderate heat until completely crispy. Set aside the bacon using a slotted spoon.
7. In a small bowl, whisk together the Parmesan cheese, eggs, egg yolks, salt, and black pepper.
8. In a large saucepan, heat the reserved pasta water over low heat.
9. Gradually introduce the egg blend into the hot pasta water, while continuously stirring with a whisk.
10. Cook until the mixture thickens, about two to three minutes.
11. In a sizable bowl, put together the prepared pasta, carbonara sauce, bacon, and parsley. Toss to evenly coat.
12. Serve hot and garnish with additional Parmesan cheese and black pepper, if desired.

4.18. AGNOLOTTI

1. Spinach and Ricotta Agnolotti

Ingredients:
- 1 pound of fresh agnolotti
- 1 cup fresh spinach leaves, chopped
- 1 cup ricotta cheese
- 1/2 cup freshly grated Parmesan cheese

- 1 egg
- Salt and black pepper, to taste
- 2 tablespoons unsalted butter
- 2 cloves of garlic, minced
- 1/4 cup chicken or vegetable broth

Instructions:
1. In a bowl, mix together the chopped spinach, ricotta cheese, grated Parmesan cheese, egg, salt, and pepper.
2. Spoon a small amount of the mixture into each agnolotti.
3. Fill a large pot with water, add a little bit of salt, and boil.
4. Once the water is boiling, add the agnolotti. Stir the pasta to prevent it from sticking together.
5. Cook the agnolotti for about three to four minutes or until it is al dente.
6. In a saucepan, melt the butter over medium temperature. Add chopped garlic and prepared for approximately one minute or until fragrant.
7. Pour in the chicken or vegetable broth and boil.
8. Reduce to low heat and allow the sauce to cook for two to three minutes, or until it has thickened slightly.
9. Drain the cooked agnolotti and add it to the saucepan. Toss to coat the pasta evenly with the sauce.
10. Serve hot, garnished with additional Parmesan cheese and fresh basil, if desired.

2. Pesto and Sun-Dried Tomato Agnolotti

Ingredients:
- 1 pound of Agnolotti pasta
- 1/2 cup basil pesto
- 1/2 cup sun-dried tomatoes, chopped
- 1/4 cup grated Parmesan cheese

- 1/4 cup heavy cream
- 2 tablespoons olive oil
- 4 cloves of garlic, minced
- Salt and pepper, to taste

Instructions:

1. Fill a large pot with water, add salt, and bring to a boil.
2. Once the water is boiling, add the agnolotti pasta and cook for about eight to ten minutes or until it is al dente.
3. Drain and rinse the pasta in cold water.
4. Warm the olive oil in a large skillet over medium temperature.
5. Add the chopped garlic and simmer for one minute, or until fragrant.
6. Stir in the sun-dried tomatoes, pesto, heavy cream, and grated Parmesan cheese.
7. Season the sauce with salt and pepper to taste.
8. In a large bowl, combine the cooked agnolotti pasta with the sauce. Toss to evenly coat the pasta.
9. Serve hot and garnish with additional Parmesan cheese and basil, if desired.
10. Enjoy your delicious Pesto and Sun-Dried Tomato Agnolotti!

4.18. AGNOLOTTI

3. Butternut Squash and Sage Agnolotti

Ingredients:
- 9 ounces agnolotti pasta
- 1 small seeded, butternut squash, diced and peeled.
- 2 tablespoons unsalted butter
- 1 tablespoon olive oil
- 2 cloves garlic, minced
- 2 tablespoons chopped fresh sage
- 1/4 cup grated Parmesan cheese
- Salt and black pepper to taste

Instructions:
1. Fill a large pot with water, add salt, and bring to a boil.
2. Once the water is boiling, add the agnolotti pasta and cook for about eight to ten minutes or until it is al dente.
3. While the agnolotti is cooking, heat the selected olive oil and butter in a sizable saucepan over moderate heat. Add the butternut squash and sauté for about eight to ten minutes, or until the squash is tender and lightly browned.
4. Add the garlic and sage to the skillet and sauté for another one to two minutes, or until fragrant.
5. Drain the agnolotti and add it to the skillet with the butternut squash mixture. Toss to combine and cook for another one to two minutes, or until the agnolotti is heated through.
6. Remove the skillet from the heat and sprinkle the grated Parmesan cheese over the top. Sprinkle with black pepper and salt to taste.
7. Serve the butternut squash and sage agnolotti immediately, garnished with additional grated Parmesan cheese and chopped fresh sage if desired. Enjoy!

4. Mushroom and Thyme Agnolotti

Ingredients:
- 1 pound of fresh agnolotti
- 8 ounces baby bella mushrooms, chopped
- 1/2 cup finely chopped onion
- 3 cloves of garlic, minced
- 1/2 teaspoon dried thyme
- Salt and black pepper, to taste
- 1/2 cup white wine
- 1/2 cup heavy cream
- 1/2 cup freshly grated Parmesan cheese

Instructions:

1. In a large skillet, heat a drizzle of olive oil over medium heat. Add chopped mushrooms, onion, minced garlic, dried thyme, salt, and pepper. Cook until the mushrooms are tender, and the onion is translucent, about five minutes.
2. Add the white wine, then simmer for two to three minutes, or until it has reduced by half.
3. Stir in the shredded Parmesan cheese as well as the heavy cream. Prepare until the sauce has thickened slightly, about five minutes.
4. Fill a large pot with water, add a little bit of salt, and boil.
5. Once the water is boiling, add the agnolotti. Stir the pasta to prevent it from sticking together.
6. Cook the agnolotti for about three to four minutes or until it is al dente.
7. Drain the cooked agnolotti and add it to the saucepan. Toss to coat the pasta evenly with the sauce.
8. Serve hot, garnished with additional Parmesan cheese and fresh thyme, if desired.

4.19. ROTINI

1. Classic Rotini Pasta Salad

Ingredients:
- 1 pound rotini pasta
- 1 cup cherry tomatoes, halved
- 1 cup cucumber, diced
- 1 cup red onion, diced
- 1 cup black olives, sliced
- 1 cup feta cheese, crumbled
- 1/2 cup Italian dressing

Instructions:
1. Fill a large pot with water, add a little bit of salt, and boil.
2. Once the water is boiling, add the rotini pasta. Stir the pasta to prevent it from sticking together.
3. Cook the rotini pasta for about eight to ten minutes or until it is al dente.
4. To test if the pasta is al dente, remove a piece of pasta from the pot and bite into it. The pasta should be cooked but still firm.
5. Drain and rinse with cold water. Set aside.
6. In a sizable saucepan, stir together the prepared rotini pasta, cherry tomatoes, cucumber, red onion, black olives, and feta cheese.
7. Drizzle with Italian dressing and mix well to combine.
8. Place it in the fridge for at least two hours before serving.

2. Rotini and Vegetable Stir-Fry

Ingredients:
- 8 ounces rotini pasta
- 2 tablespoons vegetable oil
- 1 red bell pepper, sliced
- 1 yellow bell pepper, sliced
- 1 small onion, sliced
- 2 cloves garlic, minced
- 1 tablespoon grated ginger
- 1 zucchini, sliced
- 1 yellow squash, sliced
- 1/2 teaspoon salt
- 1/4 teaspoon black pepper
- 1 tablespoon soy sauce
- 1 tablespoon honey
- 1 tablespoon cornstarch
- 1/2 cup vegetable broth
- 2 green onions, sliced

Instructions:

1. Fill a large pot with water, add a little bit of salt, and boil.
2. Once the water is boiling, add the rotini pasta. Stir the pasta to prevent it from sticking together.
3. Cook the rotini pasta for about eight to ten minutes or until it is al dente.
4. In a sizable pot or frying pan, heat the vegetable oil over medium-high heat.
5. Add the red and yellow bell peppers, onion, garlic, and ginger. Stir while frying for two to three minutes until the veggies are slightly softened.
6. Add the zucchini and yellow squash to the saucepan and stir while frying for an additional two to three minutes.
7. Season the vegetables with salt and black pepper.
8. In a tiny dish, stir together the vegetable stock, corn starch, soy sauce, and honey.
9. Layer the soy sauce blend over the veggies and stir-fry for another one to two minutes until the sauce thickens.
10. Add the cooked rotini pasta to the pan and toss with the vegetables and sauce.
11. Garnish with chopped fresh onions and serve while hot.
12. Enjoy your delicious Rotini and Vegetable Stir-Fry!

4.19. ROTINI

3. Rotini and Meatball Casserole

Ingredients:

- 1 pound rotini pasta
- 1 cup marinara sauce
- 1 cup beef broth
- 1/2 cup grated Parmesan cheese
- 1/2 cup heavy cream
- 1 cup cooked meatballs
- 1 cup mozzarella cheese, shredded
- Salt and pepper, to taste

Instructions:

1. Fill a large pot with water, add a little bit of salt, and boil.
2. Once the water is boiling, add the rotini pasta. Stir the pasta to prevent it from sticking together.
3. Cook the rotini pasta for about eight to ten minutes or until it is al dente.
4. To test if the pasta is al dente, remove a piece of pasta from the pot and bite into it. The pasta should be cooked but still firm.
5. Drain and rinse with cold water. Set aside.
6. Preheat oven to 350°F.
7. In a large saucepan, heat marinara sauce, beef broth, Parmesan cheese, and heavy cream over medium heat until well combined and heated through.
8. In a 9x13 inch baking dish, layer half of the cooked rotini pasta, half of the sauce mixture, and half of the cooked meatballs. Repeat the layering with the remaining rotini pasta, sauce mixture, and meatballs.
9. Top with mozzarella cheese and bake in the oven for twenty to twenty-five minutes or until the cheese is melted and bubbly.
10. Serve hot.

4. Creamy Rotini and Chicken Bake

Ingredients:

- 1 pound rotini pasta
- 1 cup heavy cream
- 1 cup chicken broth
- 1/2 cup grated Parmesan cheese
- 1/2 cup shredded cheddar cheese
- 1 teaspoon garlic powder
- 1 teaspoon dried basil
- 2 cups cooked and shredded chicken
- Salt and pepper, to taste

Instructions:

1. Fill a large pot with water, add a little bit of salt, and boil.
2. Once the water is boiling, add the rotini pasta. Stir the pasta to prevent it from sticking together.
3. Cook the rotini pasta for about eight to ten minutes or until it is al dente.
4. To test if the pasta is al dente, remove a piece of pasta from the pot and bite into it. The pasta should be cooked but still firm.
5. Drain and rinse with cold water. Set aside.
6. Preheat oven to 375°F.
7. In a large saucepan, heat heavy cream, chicken broth, Parmesan cheese, cheddar cheese, garlic powder, and dried basil over medium heat until well combined and heated through.
8. In a 9x13 inch baking dish, layer half of the cooked rotini pasta, half of the sauce mixture, and half of the cooked and shredded chicken. Repeat the layering with the remaining rotini pasta, sauce mixture, and chicken.
9. Place the dish in the oven and bake for twenty to twenty-five minutes, or until warmed through and all the cheese is completely melted.
10. Serve hot.

4.20. CONCHIGLIE (SHELLS)

1. Baked Stuffed Conchiglie

Ingredients:

- 1 pound large pasta conchiglie
- 1 pound ricotta cheese
- 2 cups shredded mozzarella cheese
- 1/2 cup grated Parmesan cheese
- 1 egg
- 1 tablespoon chopped fresh parsley
- 1/2 teaspoon salt
- 1/4 teaspoon black pepper
- 3 cups tomato sauce

Instructions:

1. Preheat the oven to 375°F.
2. Fill a large pot with water, add a little bit of salt, and boil.
3. Once the water is boiling, add the conchiglie pasta. Stir the pasta to prevent it from sticking together.
4. Cook the conchiglie pasta for about eight to ten minutes or until it is al dente.
5. Drain and set aside.
6. In a bowl, mix the ricotta cheese, 1 1/2 cups of the mozzarella cheese, Parmesan cheese, egg, parsley, salt, and pepper.
7. Stuff each shell with the cheese mixture and place them in a baking dish.
8. Pour the tomato sauce over the conchiglie and sprinkle with the remaining 1/2 cup of mozzarella cheese.
9. Place the dish in the oven and bake for twenty to twenty-five minutes, or until the cheese is completely melted and bubbling.

2. Creamy Conchiglie with Spinach and Bacon

Ingredients:

- 1 pound large pasta conchiglie
- 6 slices bacon, chopped
- 4 cloves garlic, minced
- 6 cups fresh spinach
- 1 cup heavy cream
- 1/2 cup grated Parmesan cheese
- Salt and pepper, to taste

Instructions:

1. Fill a large pot with water, add a little bit of salt, and boil.
2. Once the water is boiling, add the conchiglie pasta. Stir the pasta to prevent it from sticking together.

3. Cook the conchiglie pasta for about eight to ten minutes or until it is al dente. Drain and set aside.

4. In a sizable saucepan, prepare the bacon over moderate heat until crispy. Remove the bacon and set aside.

5. In the same skillet, add the sliced spinach and chopped garlic and sauté until the spinach is completely wilted.

6. Stir in the thick cream and shredded Parmesan cheese until the cheese has completely melted and the boiling sauce has thickened.

7. Add the cooked conchiglie and the bacon to the skillet and toss until everything is well combined.

8. Season with salt and pepper to taste.

4.20. CONCHIGLIE (SHELLS)

3. Stovetop Conchiglie and Cheese

Ingredients:
- 1 pound large pasta conchiglie
- 1/4 cup unsalted butter
- 1/4 cup all-purpose flour
- 2 cups whole milk
- 1 cup heavy cream
- 4 cups shredded cheddar cheese
- 1/2 teaspoon salt
- 1/4 teaspoon black pepper

Instructions:
1. Fill a large pot with water, add a little bit of salt, and boil.
2. Once the water is boiling, add the conchiglie pasta. Stir the pasta to prevent it from sticking together.
3. Cook the conchiglie pasta for about eight to ten minutes or until it is al dente. Drain and set aside.
4. In a large wok, melt the selected butter over moderate heat. Pour in the flour and sauté for one to two minutes, stirring constantly.
5. Gradually whisk in the milk and cream and continue preparing, stirring continuously, or till the sauce develops a thick texture.
6. Add the shredded cheddar cheese, salt, and black pepper and stir until the cheese is melted and the sauce is smooth.
7. Add the cooked conchiglie to the saucepan and stir until the conchiglie are coated with the cheese sauce.
8. Serve immediately.

CHAPTER 5:
VEGAN RECIPES FOR PASTA

5.1. SPAGHETTI WITH VEGAN MEATBALLS

1. Classic Vegan Meatballs

Ingredients:

- 1 pound spaghetti
- 2 cups finely chopped mushrooms
- 1/2 cup breadcrumbs
- 1/4 cup chopped fresh parsley
- 1/4 cup nutritional yeast
- 1 teaspoon dried oregano

- 1 teaspoon garlic powder
- 1/2 teaspoon salt
- 1/4 teaspoon black pepper
- 1/2 cup all-purpose flour
- 1/2 cup water
- 2 tablespoons olive oil

Instructions:

1. Fill a large saucepan with four quarts of water and let it boil.
2. Add two teaspoons of salt and two tablespoons of olive oil to the boiling water.
3. Carefully add the spaghetti to the pot and prepare for eight to ten minutes or until firm or al dente.
4. In a large bowl, combine the chopped mushrooms, breadcrumbs, parsley, nutritional yeast, oregano, garlic powder, salt, and black pepper.
5. Add the flour and mix well.
6. Gradually add water and mix until the mixture is moist and holds together.
7. Use a cookie scoop or spoon to shape the mixture into one-and-a-half-inch size balls.
8. Heat olive oil in a sizable skillet over medium heat.
9. Add the meatballs and cook for five to seven minutes, or until browned on all sides.
10. Serve the vegan meatballs over spaghetti and garnish with fresh parsley, if desired.

2. Vegan Meatballs with Quinoa

Ingredients:

- 1 pound spaghetti
- 1 cup cooked and cooled quinoa
- 1 cup cooked and mashed chickpeas
- 1/2 cup grated carrots
- 1/2 cup diced onion

- 1/4 cup breadcrumbs
- 2 tablespoons olive oil
- 2 cloves of garlic, minced
- 2 tablespoons nutritional yeast
- 1 teaspoon dried basil
- 1 teaspoon dried oregano
- Salt and pepper to taste

Instructions:

1. Fill a large saucepan with four quarts of water and let it boil.
2. Add two teaspoons of salt and two tablespoons of olive oil to the boiling water.
3. Carefully add the spaghetti to the pot and prepare for eight to ten minutes or until firm or al dente.
4. Preheat oven to 375°F. Line completely a baking sheet with parchment or grease with cooking spray.
5. In a sizable dish, combine the onions, basil, quinoa, salt, chickpeas, carrots, breadcrumbs, olive oil, garlic, nutritional yeast, oregano, and pepper. Mix well.
6. Using your hands, form the mixture into one- to two-inch (2.5-5 cm) balls. Put the formed balls onto the already made parchment covered baking sheet.
7. Bake for twenty to twenty-five minutes or until the meatballs are completely golden brown as well as crispy.
8. While the meatballs are cooking, cook the spaghetti according to the package instructions.
9. Serve the spaghetti with the vegan meatballs and your favorite pasta sauce. Enjoy!

3. Vegan Meatballs with Chickpeas

Ingredients:

- 1 pound spaghetti
- 1 cup canned chickpeas, drained and mashed
- 1/2 cup breadcrumbs
- 1/4 cup chopped fresh parsley
- 1/4 cup nutritional yeast
- 1 teaspoon dried oregano
- 1 teaspoon garlic powder
- 1/2 teaspoon salt
- 1/4 teaspoon black pepper
- 1/2 cup all-purpose flour
- 1/2 cup water
- 2 tablespoons olive oil

Instructions:

1. Fill a large saucepan with four quarts of water and let it boil.
2. Add two teaspoons of salt and two tablespoons of olive oil to the boiling water.
3. Carefully add the spaghetti to the pot and prepare for eight to ten minutes or until firm or al dente.
4. In a large bowl, combine the mashed chickpeas, breadcrumbs, parsley, nutritional yeast, oregano, garlic powder, salt, and black pepper.
5. Add the flour and mix well.
6. Gradually add water and mix until the mixture is moist and holds together.
7. Use a cookie scoop or spoon to shape the mixture into one-and-a-half-inch size balls.
8. Heat olive oil in a sizable skillet over medium heat.
9. Add the meatballs and cook for five to seven minutes, or until browned on all sides.
10. Serve the vegan meatballs over spaghetti and garnish with fresh parsley, if desired.

5.2. FETTUCCINE WITH VEGAN ALFREDO SAUCE

1. Classic Vegan Alfredo Sauce

Ingredients:
- 8 ounces fettuccine pasta
- 2 cups unsweetened almond milk
- 2 cloves of garlic, minced
- 1/2 cup raw cashews
- 1/4 cup nutritional yeast
- 2 tablespoons lemon juice
- 2 tablespoons olive oil
- Salt and black pepper, to taste

Instructions:
1. Fill a large saucepan with four quarts of water and let it boil.
2. Add one tablespoon of salt to the boiling water.
3. Add one pound of fettuccine to the pot and stir occasionally to prevent clumping.
4. Prepare the fettuccine pasta until it firms or al dente, which means it should be tender but still firm to the bite. Fresh fettuccine typically takes about two to three minutes to cook, while dried fettuccine may take up to eight minutes. Drain and set aside.
5. In a food processing machine or blender, combine the almond milk, garlic, cashews, nutritional yeast, lemon juice, olive oil, salt, and black pepper. Blend until smooth and creamy.
6. In a sizable pot over moderate heat, put in the vegan Alfredo sauce. Cook for at least five to seven minutes, stirring periodically until heated through.
7. Add the cooked fettuccine pasta to the saucepan and toss well until the pasta is evenly coated with the sauce.
8. Serve the fettuccine with classic vegan Alfredo sauce immediately, garnished with fresh herbs or grated Parmesan cheese if desired.
9. Enjoy your delicious and creamy fettuccine with classic vegan Alfredo sauce!

2. Vegan Alfredo Sauce with Cashews

Ingredients:
- 8 ounces fettuccine pasta
- 1 1/2 cups raw cashews
- 3 cloves garlic
- 1 1/2 cups vegetable broth
- 1/2 cup unsweetened almond milk

- 1/2 lemon, juiced
- 1 teaspoon salt
- 1/2 teaspoon black pepper
- 2 tablespoons nutritional yeast

- 1/4 cup freshly grated Parmesan cheese (optional)
- Fresh parsley or basil for garnish (optional)

Instructions:

1. Fill a large saucepan with four quarts of water and let it boil.
2. Add one tablespoon of salt to the boiling water.
3. Add one pound of fettuccine to the pot and stir occasionally to prevent clumping.
4. Prepare the fettuccine pasta until it firms or al dente, which means it should be tender but still firm to the bite. Fresh fettuccine typically takes about two to three minutes to cook, while dried fettuccine may take up to eight minutes.
5. Reserve 1/2 cup or bowl of the pasta liquid. Drain and set aside.
6. In a modern blender or food processing machine, add the cashews, garlic, vegetable broth, almond milk, lemon juice, salt, pepper, and nutritional yeast. Blend until smooth and creamy, about two to three minutes.
7. Pour the sauce into a skillet, then cook it while occasionally stirring over moderate heat.
8. In case the sauce seems thick, loosen with a little of the reserved pasta water until it reaches the desired consistency.
9. Stir in the Parmesan cheese, if using.
10. Toss the cooked fettuccine with the sauce and mix well.
11. Serve hot, garnished with fresh parsley or basil, if desired.
12. Enjoy your delicious and creamy vegan Alfredo sauce with fettuccine pasta!

5.2. FETTUCCINE WITH VEGAN ALFREDO SAUCE

3. Vegan Alfredo Sauce with Tofu

Ingredients:
- 1 pound fettuccine pasta
- 14 ounces firm tofu
- 1 cup unsweetened almond milk
- 1 cup cashews, soaked in water for 4 hours or overnight
- 1/2 cup nutritional yeast
- 3 cloves garlic, minced
- 2 tablespoons lemon juice
- 2 tablespoons olive oil
- Salt and pepper, to taste

Instructions:
1. Fill a large saucepan with four quarts of water and let it boil.
2. Add two tablespoons of salt to the boiling water.
3. Add one pound of fettuccine to the pot and stir occasionally to prevent clumping.
4. Prepare the fettuccine pasta until it firms or al dente, which means it should be tender but still firm to the bite. Fresh fettuccine typically takes about two to three minutes to cook, while dried fettuccine may take up to eight minutes.
5. Drain and set aside.
6. In a clean blender or food processing machine, combine the soaked cashews, almond milk, nutritional yeast, garlic, lemon juice, olive oil, salt, and pepper. Blend until smooth.
7. Crumble the tofu into a large pan and cook over medium heat until slightly browned.
8. Pour the blender mixture over the tofu in the pan and stir to combine.
9. Cook for five to seven minutes, until heated through and the sauce has thickened slightly.
10. Serve the vegan Alfredo sauce over the cooked fettuccine and enjoy!

5.3. PENNE WITH VEGAN PESTO

1. Classic Vegan Basil Pesto

Ingredients:
- 8 ounces of penne pasta
- 2 cups of fresh basil leaves
- 1/2 cup of toasted pine nuts
- 2 cloves of garlic
- 1/2 cup of olive oil

- 2 tablespoons of lemon juice
- 1/4 teaspoon of salt
- 1/4 teaspoon of black pepper
- 1/2 cup of grated vegan Parmesan cheese (optional)

Instructions:
1. Fill a large pot with water, add a pinch of salt, and bring to a boil.
2. Once the water is boiling, add the homemade penne pasta. Stir the pasta to prevent it from sticking together.
3. Cook the penne pasta for about eight to ten minutes or until it is al dente.
4. To test if the pasta is al dente, remove a piece of pasta from the pot and bite into it. The pasta should be cooked but still firm.
5. As soon as the pasta is ready, in a colander, drain and rinse it with cold water.
6. While the pasta is cooking, make the pesto. In a food processing machine, combine the chopped garlic, basil leaves, toasted pine nuts, olive oil, lemon juice, salt, and pepper.
7. Process until the mixture is smooth.
8. As soon as the pasta is ready, drain it and put it back into the pot.
9. Add the pesto to the pot and mix until the pasta is fully coated.
10. If desired, add the grated vegan Parmesan cheese and mix until it is melted and evenly distributed.
11. Serve hot and enjoy!

Note: You can also add some cherry tomatoes, roasted red peppers, or chopped walnuts to the dish for added flavor and texture.

5.3. PENNE WITH VEGAN PESTO

2. Vegan Pesto with Spinach and Walnuts

Ingredients:
- 1 cup fresh basil leaves
- 2 cups fresh spinach leaves
- 1/2 cup walnuts
- 1/2 cup extra virgin olive oil
- 4 garlic cloves

- 1/2 lemon, juiced
- Salt and pepper to taste
- 1 pound penne pasta
- 1/2 cup vegan Parmesan cheese (optional)

Instructions:
1. Fill a large pot with water, add a pinch of salt, and bring to a boil.
2. Once the water is boiling, add the homemade penne pasta. Stir the pasta to prevent it from sticking together.
3. Cook the penne pasta for about eight to ten minutes or until it is al dente.
4. To test if the pasta is al dente, remove a piece of pasta from the pot and bite into it. The pasta should be cooked but still firm.
5. Reserve 1/2 cup of pasta water. Drain and set aside.
6. In a food processor, add the basil, spinach, walnuts, garlic, lemon juice, salt, and pepper. Pulse until the mixture is finely chopped.
7. Slowly pour in the olive oil while continuing to pulse until the mixture is smooth and well combined.
8. Stir in the vegan Parmesan cheese (if using).
9. Toss the cooked penne pasta with the pesto sauce until well coated. If the sauce is too thick, loosen it by adding water from the reserved pasta.
10. Serve the penne with the vegan pesto with spinach and walnuts hot, garnished with extra vegan Parmesan cheese as well as a squeeze from freshly squeezed lemon juice if desired.

3. Arugula and Walnut Pesto Penne

Ingredients:
- 1 pound penne pasta
- 2 cups arugula
- 1/2 cup walnuts

- 2 garlic cloves, minced
- 1/2 cup nutritional yeast
- 1/2 cup olive oil
- Salt and pepper to taste

Instructions:

1. In a big saucepan of boiling water with salt, cook the penne pasta until firm or al dente, for approximately eight to ten minutes. Drain and set aside.
2. In a food processor, combine the arugula, walnuts, garlic, and nutritional yeast. Pulse until finely chopped.
3. While the machine [food processor] is running, gradually introduce the olive oil until the pesto is smooth and well combined.
4. Add salt and pepper to taste.
5. Toss the cooked penne with the pesto until well coated.
6. Serve immediately.

4. Vegan Pesto with Sun-Dried Tomatoes

Ingredients:

- 1 cup sun-dried tomatoes, packed in oil
- 1 cup fresh basil leaves
- 1/2 cup walnuts
- 3 cloves of garlic
- 2 tablespoons lemon juice
- 1/4 cup extra-virgin olive oil
- Salt and pepper, to taste
- 1 pound penne pasta
- 1/2 cup grated Parmesan cheese (optional)

Instructions:

1. In a food processing machine or clean blender, mix together the sun-dried tomatoes, basil, walnuts, and garlic until finely chopped.
2. While the machine [food processor] is running, gradually pour in the lemon juice and olive oil until the mixture forms a smooth paste.
3. Sprinkle the vegan pesto with pepper and salt, to taste.
4. In a big saucepan of boiling water with salt, cook the penne pasta until firm or al dente, for approximately eight to ten minutes. Drain and set aside.
5. In a large bowl, toss the cooked penne with the vegan pesto until evenly coated.
6. Serve hot and garnish with grated Parmesan cheese, if desired. Enjoy!

CHAPTER 6:
SAUCES FOR PASTA

TOMATO
SAUCE
31st May

6.1. TOMATO SAUCE

1. Classic Tomato Sauce
2. Tomato Sauce with Fresh Basil
3. Tomato Sauce with Olives and Capers
4. Tomato Sauce with Anchovies
5. Tomato Sauce with Mushrooms

Ingredients:
- 2 tablespoons olive oil
- 1 medium onion, finely chopped
- 4 garlic cloves, minced
- 1 can (14.5 ounces) crushed tomatoes
- Salt and pepper to taste
- Fresh basil, chopped (for the basil variation)
- 1/2 cup black olives, pitted and chopped (for the olives and capers variation)
- 2 tablespoons capers, drained (for the olives and capers variation)
- 6 anchovy fillets, chopped (for the anchovy variation)
- 1 cup sliced mushrooms (for the mushroom variation)

Instructions:
1. Fill a large pot with water, add a pinch of salt, and bring to a boil.
2. Once the water is boiling, add the homemade penne pasta. Stir the pasta to prevent it from sticking together.
3. Cook the penne pasta for about eight to ten minutes or until it is al dente.
4. To test if the pasta is al dente, remove a piece of pasta from the pot and bite into it. The pasta should be cooked but still firm.
5. Reserve 1/2 cup of pasta water. Drain and set aside.
6. In a food processor, add the basil, spinach, walnuts, garlic, lemon juice, salt, and pepper. Pulse until the mixture is finely chopped.
7. Slowly pour in the olive oil while continuing to pulse until the mixture is smooth and well combined.
8. Stir in the vegan Parmesan cheese (if using).
9. Toss the cooked penne pasta with the pesto sauce until well coated. If the sauce is too thick, loosen it by adding water from the reserved pasta.
10. Serve the penne with the vegan pesto with spinach and walnuts hot, garnished with extra vegan Parmesan cheese as well as a squeeze from freshly squeezed lemon juice if desired.

6.2. PESTO SAUCE

1. Classic Basil Pesto
2. Spinach Pesto
3. Arugula Pesto
4. Sun-Dried Tomato Pesto
5. Walnut Pesto

Ingredients:

- 2 cups fresh basil leaves (for Classic Basil Pesto)
- 2 cups fresh spinach leaves (for Spinach Pesto)
- 2 cups fresh arugula leaves (for Arugula Pesto)
- 1/2 cup sun-dried tomatoes (for Sun-Dried Tomato Pesto)
- 1/2 cup walnuts (for Walnut Pesto)
- 1/2 cup freshly grated Parmesan cheese
- 1/2 cup extra virgin olive oil
- 4 cloves of garlic
- Salt and pepper, to taste

Instructions:

1. Combine the chosen leaves (basil, spinach, arugula, or a combination) in a food processor or blender.
2. Add in sun-dried tomatoes (for Sun-Dried Tomato Pesto) or walnuts (for Walnut Pesto), Parmesan cheese, and garlic.
3. With the processor running, slowly add in the extra virgin olive oil until the mixture becomes smooth and well combined.
4. Season with salt and pepper to taste.
5. If desired, add more olive oil for a smoother consistency.
6. Reserve the pesto in an airtight container and place in the fridge for up to five days or freeze for later use.
7. Enjoy with pasta, spread on bread, or use as a dip or sauce for meats and vegetables.

6.3. ALFREDO SAUCE

1. Classic Alfredo Sauce
2. Alfredo Sauce with Broccoli
3. Alfredo Sauce with Spinach
4. Alfredo Sauce with Chicken
5. Alfredo Sauce with Shrimp

Ingredients:

- 2 cups heavy cream
- 1 cup grated Parmesan cheese
- 1/2 cup unsalted butter
- 2 cloves of garlic, minced
- Salt and pepper, to taste
- Optional: 1 cup cooked and chopped broccoli, spinach, chicken, or shrimp

Instructions:

1. In a sizable saucepan, warm the thick cream along with the butter over moderate heat till the butter is melted and the mixture starts to simmer.
2. Add the chopped garlic and mix for approximately one to two minutes, or until fragrant.
3. Reduce to low heat and gently add the grated Parmesan cheese, whisking constantly till the cheese is completely melted and the cooked sauce is smooth.
4. Sprinkle the sauce with pepper and salt, to taste.
5. If desired, add in the optional ingredients (broccoli, spinach, chicken, or shrimp) and stir until heated through.
6. Serve the sauce immediately over pasta or as desired.

6.4. VODKA SAUCE

1. Classic Vodka Sauce
2. Vodka Sauce with Tomatoes and Basil
3. Vodka Sauce with Spinach and Ricotta
4. Vodka Sauce with Shrimp
5. Vodka Sauce with Chicken

Ingredients:
- 2 tablespoons unsalted butter
- 1 cup heavy cream
- 1/2 cup vodka
- 2 cloves garlic, minced
- 1 can (14.5 ounces) crushed tomatoes or 2 large fresh tomatoes, diced
- 2 tablespoons chopped fresh basil
- 2 tablespoons chopped fresh spinach
- 1/4 cup ricotta cheese
- 1 cup cooked chopped chicken or shrimp
- Salt and pepper to taste
- 1 pound penne pasta, cooked al dente
- Grated Parmesan cheese, for serving (optional)

Instructions:
1. In a sizable pot, melt the selected butter over moderate heat. Add the chopped garlic and sauté for at least one minute or until fragrant.
2. Put in the vodka and thick cream and stir to combine. Boil, then take down the heat to low and let simmer for two to three minutes.
3. If using canned tomatoes, add them to the saucepan and stir to combine. If using fresh tomatoes, add them in after step five.
4. If using the basil, spinach, and ricotta, add them now and stir to combine. Let the sauce simmer for five to seven minutes, until it has thickened slightly.
5. If using the chicken or shrimp, add it to the saucepan and stir to combine. Let the sauce simmer for another two to three minutes.
6. Season the sauce with salt and pepper to taste.
7. Dish the sauce over cooked penne pasta and sprinkle with grated Parmesan cheese, if desired.

6.5. CARBONARA SAUCE

1. Classic Carbonara Sauce
2. Carbonara Sauce with Broccoli
3. Carbonara Sauce with Spinach
4. Carbonara Sauce with Shrimp
5. Carbonara Sauce with Chicken

Ingredients:

- 1 pound spaghetti or other pasta of choice
- 1 cup pancetta or bacon, diced
- 8 ounces heavy cream
- 4 cloves garlic, minced
- 4 large egg yolks
- 1 cup grated Parmesan cheese
- Salt and pepper, to taste
- 1 cup broccoli florets (for Carbonara Sauce with Broccoli variation)
- 1 cup packed spinach leaves (for Carbonara Sauce with Spinach variation)
- 1 pound peeled, medium shrimp, and deveined (meant for Carbonara Sauce with Shrimp variation)
- 1 pound boneless, skinless chicken breast, diced (for Carbonara Sauce with Chicken variation)

Instructions:

1. Cook pasta. Reserve one cup of the pasta water.
2. In a large pan, cook pancetta or bacon over medium heat until crispy. Using a slotted spoon take the pan down and set it by the side.
3. Add garlic to the pan and cook for one to two minutes until fragrant. Remove from heat.
4. In a large bowl, whisk together the heavy cream, egg yolks, Parmesan cheese, salt, and pepper.
5. Add the cooked pasta to the bowl with the sauce mixture, tossing to coat.
6. If making the Carbonara Sauce with Broccoli variation, steam broccoli florets until tender, about five minutes. Add to the pasta mixture.
7. If making the Carbonara Sauce with Spinach variation, add the packed spinach leaves to the pasta mixture.
8. If making the Carbonara Sauce with Shrimp variation, add the cooked shrimp to the pasta mixture.
9. If making the Carbonara Sauce with Chicken variation, add the cooked chicken to the pasta mixture.
10. In case the pasta looks too dry, moisten by adding a little bit of the reserved pasta water to loosen the sauce.
11. Serve hot, garnished with the reserved pancetta or bacon.

6.6. PUTTANESCA SAUCE

**1. Classic Puttanesca Sauce
2. Puttanesca Sauce with Olives and Capers
3. Puttanesca Sauce with Anchovies
4. Puttanesca Sauce with Shrimp
5. Puttanesca Sauce with Chicken**

Ingredients:

- ·1/2 cup chopped onion
- ·4 cloves of garlic, minced
- ·2 tablespoons olive oil
- ·2 cans of crushed tomatoes
- ·1 teaspoon salt
- ·1 teaspoon black pepper
- ·1 teaspoon dried oregano
- ·1 teaspoon dried basil
- ·1/2 teaspoon red pepper flakes (optional)
- ·1/2 cup chopped kalamata olives
- ·1/4 cup capers
- ·4 anchovy fillets, chopped
- ·1 pound cooked, peeled, and deveined shrimp (optional)
- ·1 pound cooked, diced chicken (optional)

Instructions:

1. In a sizable pot, warm the olive oil over medium temperature.
2. Add the sliced onion and chopped garlic and prepare until softened, about five minutes.
3. Stir in the crushed tomatoes, salt, pepper, oregano, basil, and red pepper flakes.
4. Bring the mixture [sauce] to a boiling and let it cook for ten minutes.
5. Stir in the olives, capers, and anchovy fillets. Cook for five minutes.
6. If using shrimp or chicken, add it to the sauce and cook until heated through, about five minutes.
7. Serve the sauce over pasta of your choice.

Note: You can use one of the variations, or a combination of them, as desired. The classic puttanesca sauce is made without any seafood or meat.

CHAPTER 7:
TOPPINGS FOR PASTA

7.1. Grated Cheese Toppings

When it comes to grated cheese toppings, there are hundreds of options to select from, each one with its own unique flavor and texture. Here are a few popular grated cheese options to consider:

1.Parmesan Cheese

Parmesan cheese is a hard, salty cheese that originated in the Parma region of Italy. It's commonly used as a topping for pasta dishes and has a nutty, earthy flavor that pairs well with many pasta sauces. It's important to note that not all Parmesan cheese is created equal, as some may contain fillers like cellulose powder. Be sure to look for a high-quality, freshly grated Parmesan cheese for the best taste and texture.

2.Pecorino Romano Cheese

Pecorino Romano cheese is another hard, salty cheese that is often used in pasta dishes. Unlike Parmesan cheese, Pecorino Romano cheese is made from sheep's milk and has a stronger, saltier flavor. It's a versatile cheese that can be used in a variety of pasta dishes, but it's especially good as a topping for tomato-based sauces.

3.Grana Padano Cheese

Grana Padano cheese is a semi-hard cheese that is similar to Parmesan cheese, but it has a milder, creamier flavor. It's a great cheese for those who prefer a more subtle flavor in their pasta toppings, and it's also an affordable alternative to Parmesan cheese. Grana Padano cheese can be shaved or grated, and it's an excellent choice for those who are looking to add a little extra creaminess to their pasta dishes.

4.Asiago Cheese

Asiago is a hard, nutty, and slightly sharp cheese that originates from the Veneto region of Italy. It is made from cow's milk and has a slightly crumbly texture. When grated, it can be used as a topping for pasta dishes, salads, and soups. It pairs well with pasta dishes that have a mild flavor and can add a depth of flavor to tomato-based sauces.

5. Gorgonzola Cheese

Gorgonzola cheese is a category of blue-like cheeses that are produced in the Piedmont and Lombardy regions of Italy. It has a creamy, tangy flavor with a slightly pungent aroma. When grated, it can be used as a topping for pasta dishes, salads, and soups. It pairs well with pasta dishes that have bold flavors, such as spicy or tomato-based sauces.

6.Feta Cheese

Feta is a type of brined curd cheese that originates from Greece. It has a tangy, salty flavor and a crumbly texture. When grated, it can be used as a topping for pasta dishes, salads, and soups. It pairs well with pasta dishes that have a light flavor, such as lemon or olive oil-based sauces. It can also be used to add a salty, tangy flavor to tomato-based sauces.

7. Gouda Cheese

Gouda cheese is a semi-firm cheese that got its origins from the Netherlands. It has a nutty and slightly sweet flavor, with a creamy texture. Gouda cheese is a great option for pasta dishes with creamy or cheesy sauces, as it melts well and adds a rich, savory flavor to the dish.

8. Ricotta Cheese

Ricotta is a creamy and soft cheese that is often used as a filling for pasta dishes like ravioli and cannelloni. It has a moderate, mildly sweet flavor that pairs well with a variety of pasta sauces, including tomato-based sauces, creamy sauces, and pesto. Ricotta cheese can also be used as a topping for baked pasta dishes.

9. Blue Cheese

Blue cheese, also known as Roquefort or Stilton, is a strong and pungent cheese that is aged with the mold Penicillium. It has a strong and salty fragrance, with a distinctive blue or green mold running through it. Blue cheese is best used sparingly as a topping for pasta dishes, as its strong flavor can easily overpower the other ingredients. It pairs well with dishes that have a strong or spicy flavor, such as buffalo chicken pasta or pasta with spicy sausage.

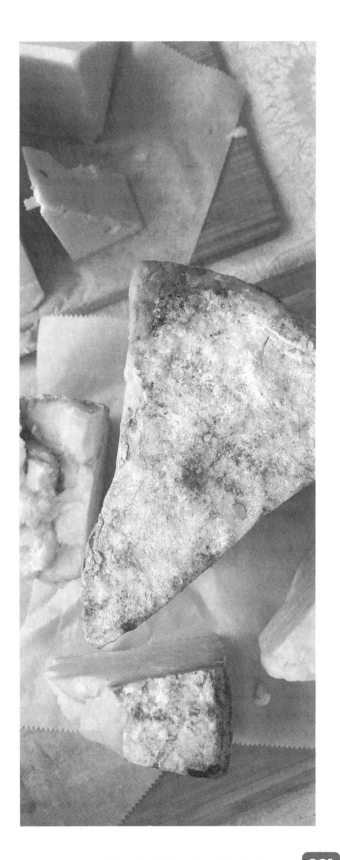

7.2. Nuts and Seeds Toppings

1. Pine Nuts

Pine nuts are small, delicate nuts with a slightly sweet, nutty flavor. They are commonly used in Mediterranean cuisine and are often added to pasta dishes as a topping. When toasted, pine nuts have a rich, buttery flavor that pairs well with pasta dishes made with cream-based sauces, as well as with tomato-based sauces.

2. Walnuts

Walnuts have a strong, earthy flavor that complements pasta dishes made with hearty sauces. They are often used in pesto, which is a classic pasta sauce made with basil, garlic, and olive oil. When toasted, walnuts have a nutty flavor that enhances the taste of pasta dishes.

3. Pistachios

Pistachios have a unique, slightly sweet flavor that pairs well with pasta dishes made with tomato-based sauces. They are often used in Mediterranean cuisine and are known for their bright green color, which adds an attractive touch to pasta dishes. When toasted, pistachios have a crunchy texture that adds a satisfying crunch to pasta dishes.

4. Almonds

Almonds are crunchy and nutty, adding a delightful texture and flavor to pasta dishes. They are very rich in protein and good fats, and fiber, making them a great addition to vegan and vegetarian pasta dishes. They can be toasted and sprinkled on top of pasta dishes or blended into sauces to add richness and creaminess.

5. Sunflower Seeds

Sunflower seeds are a versatile and nutritious seed that can be used to top pasta dishes. They are very rich in protein and good fats, and fiber, making them a great addition to vegan and vegetarian pasta dishes. Sunflower seeds have a slightly sweet and nutty flavor that pairs well with pasta dishes that contain fresh herbs, vegetables, and sauces. They can be toasted and sprinkled on top of pasta dishes or blended into sauces to add texture and flavor.

6. Pepitas (Pumpkin Seeds)

Pepitas, also known as pumpkin seeds, are a nutritious and delicious seed that can be used to top pasta dishes. They are very rich in protein and good fats, and fiber, making them a great addition to vegan and vegetarian pasta dishes. Pepitas have a slightly sweet and nutty flavor that pairs well with pasta dishes that contain fresh herbs, vegetables, and sauces. They can be toasted and sprinkled on top of pasta dishes or blended into sauces to add texture and flavor.

7. Sesame Seeds

Sesame seeds are a flavorful and nutritious seed that can be used to top pasta dishes. They are very rich in protein and good fats, and fiber, making them a great addition to vegan and vegetarian pasta dishes. Sesame seeds have a nutty and slightly sweet flavor that pairs well with pasta dishes that contain fresh herbs, vegetables, and sauces. They can be toasted and sprinkled on top of pasta dishes or blended into sauces to add texture and flavor.

7.3. Meat Toppings

1. Cooked Bacon
Bacon is a popular meat topping for pasta dishes, adding a salty and savory flavor. To cook bacon, it can be fried in a pan on medium heat until crispy. Rest on a paper napkin to remove additional grease just before topping your cooked pasta.

2. Cooked Sausage
Sausage can add a bold, spicy flavor to your pasta dish. It can be grilled, sautéed, or baked in the oven until fully cooked. Be sure to slice the sausage into rounds before adding to your pasta. You can also choose to remove the sausage from the casing before cooking and break it apart, cooking it into crumbles.

3. Cooked Chicken
Cooked chicken [especially chicken breast] is an outstanding protein source and can add a mild, savory flavor to your pasta. It can be grilled, sautéed, or baked in the oven until fully cooked. Dice the chicken into small pieces before adding to your pasta.

4. Cooked Beef
Cooked beef is a great addition to pasta dishes for those who enjoy a heartier meal. It can be added to dishes like spaghetti Bolognese or beef and mushroom fettuccine. Cooked beef can be sliced or diced, depending on the desired texture and flavor. You can also choose to use ground beef, breaking it up and cooking it into crumbles.

5. Cooked Prosciutto
Cooked prosciutto is a salty, cured ham that adds a burst of flavor to pasta dishes. It is typically sliced thin and added as a topping for pasta with lighter sauces like pesto or Alfredo.

6. Cooked Pancetta
Cooked pancetta is an Italian bacon that has a slightly sweeter and saltier taste than regular bacon. It adds a rich, savory flavor to pasta dishes and is often used in carbonara sauce. Pancetta can be diced and added to pasta dishes as a topping, or it can be fried until crispy and added as a garnish.

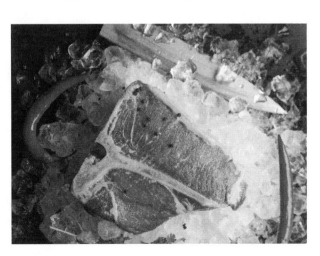

7.4. Herb and Spice Toppings

1. Fresh Basil

Fresh basil is a popular herb used in many Italian dishes. It has a sweet, slightly pungent flavor that pairs well with tomato-based sauces, pesto, and many cheese dishes. Fresh basil is a staple in many herb gardens and can be easily grown indoors or outdoors. When using fresh basil in pasta dishes, it is best to add it just before serving to maintain its flavor and aroma.

2. Oregano

Oregano is another popular Italian herb that has a warm, slightly bitter flavor. It is commonly used in pasta dishes, especially those with tomato-based sauces and meat dishes. Oregano can be used dried or fresh, but it is best to use dried oregano in long-simmering sauces, as it will release its flavor over time.

3. Red Pepper Flakes

Red-pepper shavings are made from crisped red chillies and add a spicy, slightly pungent flavor to pasta dishes. They are often sprinkled on top of finished pasta dishes, or added to sauces to provide heat and depth of flavor. Red pepper flakes can be adjusted to taste, and just a little stretches a long way, so be careful not to overuse them.

4. Fresh Parsley

Parsley is a popular herb that adds a bright, fresh flavor to pasta dishes. It can be a garnish on top of your cooked pasta or incorporated into the sauce. Fresh parsley has a light, slightly bitter taste that complements the flavors of many pasta dishes.

5. Thyme

Thyme is an herb that adds a warm, woody flavor to pasta dishes. It is often used in Mediterranean and French cuisine. Thyme pairs well with ingredients such as garlic, olive oil, and tomatoes.

6. Rosemary

Rosemary is an herb that adds a distinctive, pine-like flavor to pasta dishes. It pairs well with ingredients such as garlic, lemon, and mushrooms. Rosemary is often used in Mediterranean cuisine.

7. Sage

Sage is an herb that adds a savory, slightly bitter flavor to pasta dishes. It pairs well with ingredients such as garlic, onion, and cheese. Sage is often used in Italian and Mediterranean cuisine.

8. Chives

Chives are a type of onion that adds a mild, slightly sweet flavor to pasta dishes. They are often used as a topping for pasta or incorporated into the sauce. Chives pair well with ingredients such as cheese, sour cream, and butter.

7.5. Vegetable Toppings

1. Roasted Garlic

For the Roasted Garlic topping, you can make this by first peeling off the outer layers of the garlic bulb to reveal individual cloves. Cut off the top of each clove to expose the inside and place the cloves in a small baking dish or on a sheet of aluminum foil. Drizzle the exposed garlic with olive oil, season with salt and pepper, and wrap the foil around the cloves or cover the baking dish with foil. Bake at 400 degrees Fahrenheit in a pre-heated oven for thirty to thirty-five minutes or until the garlic is soft and lightly browned. Once done, you can mash the roasted garlic with a fork and add it to your pasta.

2. Sauteed Mushrooms

For the Sauteed Mushrooms topping, you can start by cleaning and slicing a variety of mushrooms such as button, cremini, or shiitake mushrooms. Heat a sizable saucepan over moderate-high temperature and add some olive oil. Add the chopped mushrooms and sauté until they're soft and golden brown, about five to seven minutes. You can season the mushrooms with salt, pepper, and any other herbs or spices you like. Once done, you can add the sauteed mushrooms on top of your pasta.

3. Roasted Red Peppers

For the Roasted Red Peppers topping, you can either use store-bought jarred roasted red peppers or make your own by roasting fresh red bell peppers. To make your own, preheat your oven to 450°F and place the red bell peppers on a baking sheet. Roast the peppers for about twenty to twenty-five minutes or until the skin is charred and blistered. Transfer the roasted peppers to a bowl and cover with plastic wrap for about ten minutes to let them steam. Then take the peppers' skin off, take out the seeds and stem, and cut into thin pieces. You can add the roasted red peppers on top of your pasta and sprinkle with some freshly chopped basil.

4. Grilled Eggplant

Grilled eggplant is a delicious and healthy option as a topping for pasta. The smoky and slightly sweet flavor of grilled eggplant pairs well with tomato-based pasta sauces. To prepare, slice eggplant into 1/2 inch rounds or lengthwise strips, brush with olive oil and season with salt and pepper. Grill until charred and tender, about three to five minutes per side. Serve on top of pasta dishes, such as spaghetti with marinara sauce, or as a vegetarian alternative to meat-based toppings.

5. Caramelized Onions

Caramelized onions add a sweet, rich flavor to pasta dishes. To prepare, thinly slice one to two medium onions and cook them over medium-low heat in a large pan with two tablespoons of butter or oil until they are soft and golden brown. This process can take up to thirty minutes, but the end result is worth the wait. Stir occasionally to prevent burning. Caramelized onions can be used as a topping for pasta dishes like fettuccine Alfredo or as a base for sauces such as a creamy garlic sauce.

6. Sautéed Spinach

Sautéed spinach is a nutritious and delicious topping for pasta. Rinse and dry fresh spinach, then sauté in a pan with garlic and olive oil until just wilted. Spinach is a great source of iron, making it an awesome option for those desiring to incorporate more nutrients into their diet.

7. Roasted Zucchini

Roasting zucchini is a simple way to bring out its natural sweetness and add a caramelized flavor to your pasta dish. Thinly slice a zucchini and place it on a baking sheet. Drizzle with salt, olive oil, and pepper. Roast at 400 degrees Fahrenheit in a pre-heated oven for twenty to twenty-five minutes until golden brown. The roasted zucchini will add a mild, sweet flavor and a crispy texture to your pasta dish and can be seasoned with herbs and spices to taste.

8. Grilled Asparagus

Asparagus is a very delicious as well as nutritious veggie that can be grilled to bring out its natural flavors. Grilling asparagus is quick and easy and it's a great way to add a new twist to your pasta dish. To grill asparagus, simply toss the spears with olive oil and sprinkle with pepper and salt. Then

place them on a hot grill and prepare until they are completely soft and slightly charred, about five to seven minutes. Grilled asparagus adds a fresh, crisp flavor and a nice crunch to your pasta dish.

9. Grilled Bell Peppers

Bell peppers are a staple in many pasta dishes and grilling them brings out their sweet and smoky flavors. To grill bell peppers, cut the bell peppers into thin strips, removing the stem and seeds. Gently rub with good olive oil and barbecue until tender and slightly charred, about five to seven minutes. Grilled bell peppers add a sweet, smoky flavor and a tender texture to your pasta dish.

10. Sautéed Kale

Kale is a nutritious and flavorful leafy green that can be sautéed to make a delicious topping for pasta. Wash and chop the kale, removing the tough stem. Heat a sizable saucepan over moderate heat with olive oil and add the chopped kale. Sauté until wilted, about three to five minutes. Season with salt and pepper to taste. Sautéed kale adds a slightly bitter and earthy flavor, as well as a tender texture, to your pasta dish.

CHAPTER 8:
PASTA AND WINE PAIRING

8.1. Understanding the Basics of Pasta and Wine Pairing

Pasta and wine have been enjoyed together for centuries, with the right combination elevating the flavors of both. There are a few key elements to consider when cooking pasta incorporated with wine. The first is the sauce, as this will have a big impact on the type of wine that will complement the dish. The second is the pasta shape, as different shapes are better suited to different types of sauces. Finally, the acidity and body of the wine also play a role in determining the ideal pairing.

When it comes to pasta sauces, there are three main categories: light, medium, and heavy. Light sauces, such as olive oil and garlic or tomato and basil, pair well with lighter bodied wines like pinot grigio or sauvignon blanc. Medium sauces, such as cream sauces or carbonara, pair well with medium-bodied wines like chardonnay or pinot noir. Finally, heavy sauces, such as Bolognese or Alfredo, pair well with full-bodied wines like cabernet sauvignon or syrah.

The pasta shape is also important to consider. Thinner, more delicate pasta shapes, such as angel hair or spaghetti, pair well with lighter sauces. Heartier, thicker pasta shapes, such as rigatoni or fettuccine, pair well with heavier sauces. Additionally, some pasta shapes are better suited to certain types of sauces. For example, thicker pasta shapes like penne or ziti are great for meat-based sauces, while more delicate shapes like angel hair or capellini are ideal for seafood or vegetable-based sauces.

Finally, the acidity and body of the wine play a role in the overall pairing. Acidic wines, such as sauvignon blanc, pair well with light, acidic sauces like tomato sauce. Heavier, more full-bodied wines, such as cabernet sauvignon, pair well with heavy sauces like Bolognese or Alfredo. The idea is to balance the flavors and textures of both the pasta and the wine, creating a harmonious and enjoyable dining experience.

In conclusion, pairing pasta with wine requires a bit of understanding and thought, but the reward is a delicious and memorable meal. By considering the sauce, pasta shape, and acidity and body of the wine, you can create the perfect pairing that will bring out the best in both the pasta and the wine.

8.2. Red Wine and Pasta Pairing

1. Chianti and Bolognese Sauce
Chianti is a classic red wine from Tuscany, Italy with a medium body and high acidity. The bold flavors of the Bolognese sauce, with its combination of ground beef, tomatoes, and wine, complement the fruitiness of the Chianti, making it a perfect match.

2. Pinot Noir and Pesto Sauce
Pinot noir is a light to medium-bodied red

wine with soft tannins and flavors of cherries and red fruits. The bright and fresh flavors of pesto, with its combination of basil, garlic, and pine nuts, pair well with the lighter body and fruity notes of pinot noir.

3. Merlot and Tomato Sauce

Merlot is a medium-bodied red wine with soft tannins and a velvety texture. The sweet and slightly acidic flavors of tomato sauce, with its juicy and fresh taste, pair well with the fruitiness and soft tannins of merlot.

4.Cabernet Sauvignon and Alfredo Sauce

Cabernet sauvignon is a full-bodied red wine with high tannins and bold flavors of black fruit, cassis, and oak. The richness and creaminess of Alfredo sauce, with its combination of butter, cream, and Parmesan cheese, pair well with the bold flavors and tannins of cabernet sauvignon.

8.3. White Wine and Pasta Pairing

1. Pinot Grigio with Clam Sauce

Pinot grigio is a light-bodied white wine with citrus and green apple flavors. The lightness of the wine pairs well with the salty, briny flavor of the clam sauce, creating a harmonious balance of flavors.

2. Sauvignon Blanc with Tomato and Basil Sauce

Sauvignon blanc is a crisp, refreshing wine with bright citrus and herbal notes. The acid content of the wine cuts right through the richness of the tomato sauce and complements the fresh basil flavor.

3. Chardonnay with Pesto Sauce

Chardonnay is a medium-bodied white wine with buttery and tropical fruit flavors. The richness of the wine pairs well with the creamy, nutty flavor of the pesto sauce, creating a rich, comforting dish.

4. Riesling with Carbonara Sauce

Riesling is a light-bodied wine with sweet fruit and floral notes. The sweetness of the wine complements the salty flavor of the carbonara sauce and cuts through the richness of the dish, creating a harmonious balance of flavors.

8.4. Sparkling Wine and Pasta Pairing

1. Prosecco with Tomato Sauce
The light and refreshing bubbles of prosecco complement the sweetness of ripe tomatoes in the tomato sauce. The acid content of the wine cuts right through the uniqueness of the sauce, making for a balanced and enjoyable pairing.

2. Champagne with Alfredo Sauce
The creamy, decadent texture of Alfredo sauce pairs well with the crisp, elegant bubbles of champagne. The wine's acidity provides a clean finish to the richness of the sauce, making for a luxurious and indulgent meal.

3. Sparkling Wine with Pesto Sauce
The fresh and herbaceous notes in pesto sauce pair well with the bright acidity and bubbles in sparkling wine. This is a light and refreshing pairing, perfect for summertime pasta dishes.

4. Sparkling Rosé with Shrimp Scampi
The light and delicate flavors in a shrimp scampi sauce pair perfectly with the crisp and dry notes of a sparkling rosé. The wine's lightness and acidity balance the richness of the sauce, making for a harmonious pairing.

5. Cava with Carbonara Sauce
The rich and savory flavors in a carbonara sauce pair well with the crisp and refreshing notes of Cava. The wine's acidity provides a clean finish to the richness of the sauce, making for a balanced and enjoyable meal.

6. Sparkling Wine with Puttanesca Sauce
The bold and robust flavors in a puttanesca sauce pair well with the bright and effervescent notes of sparkling wine. The wine's acidity cuts through the richness of the sauce, making for a lively and satisfying pairing.

7. Moscato d'Asti with Fresh Basil Sauce
The light and sweet notes in a moscato d'asti wine complement the bright and herbaceous flavors in a fresh basil sauce. The wine's effervescence provides a clean finish to the richness of the sauce, making for a light and refreshing pairing.

8. Asti Spumante with Tomato and Olive Sauce
The bold and juicy flavors in a tomato and olive sauce pair well with the bright and effervescent notes of asti spumante. The wine's acidity cuts through the richness of the sauce, making for a lively and satisfying pairing.

CHAPTER 9:
HOW TO FREEZE, STORE, AND DEFROST PASTA

9.1. How to Freeze Pasta

Freezing pasta is a great way to extend its shelf life and save time when preparing a meal. Here are two methods for freezing pasta:

1. Freezing Fresh Pasta
- Fresh pasta is best frozen before it is cooked.
- Allow the pasta to air-dry for about an hour after making it or purchasing it.
- Spread the dried pasta out in a single line on a baking tray coated with parchment paper or a plastic sheet.
- Freeze the pasta on the baking sheet for about one to two hours, or until it is solid.
- Once the pasta is frozen, transfer it to a freezer-safe container or a freezer-safe plastic bag.
- Label the container or bag with the date and type of pasta.
- Fresh pasta can be stored in the freezer for up to three months.

2. Freezing Cooked Pasta
- Cooked pasta can also be frozen, but it should be cooled to room temperature before freezing.
- Place the cooked pasta in a single line on a baking tray coated with parchment paper or plastic wrap.
- Freeze the pasta on the baking sheet for about one to two hours, or until it is solid.

- Once the pasta is frozen, transfer it to a freezer-safe container or a freezer-safe plastic bag.
- Label the container or bag with the date and type of pasta.
- Cooked pasta can be stored in the freezer for up to two months.

9.2. How to Store Pasta

When it comes to storing pasta, there are a few things to consider to ensure that it stays fresh and tasty. Here is more information about storing fresh and cooked pasta:

1. Storing Fresh Pasta
- Fresh pasta is best stored in the refrigerator as soon as possible after it is made. The ideal temperature for storing fresh pasta is between 33°F to 39°F.
- Wrap the pasta in plastic wrap or place it in an airtight container to ensure it doesn't dry out.
- Freshly made pasta can be preserved in the fridge for two to three days, but the texture and flavor may start to deteriorate after that.
- If you are not planning to use it within two to three days, you can freeze it for up to two months.

2. Storing Prepared Pasta
- Homemade pasta should be refrigerated in a sealed container.
- Cooked pasta is best stored within two hours of cooking.

- To prevent the pasta from sticking together, add butter or olive oil to the pasta before storing.
- Cooked pasta can last for up to five days in the refrigerator.
- If you are not planning to eat it within five days, you can freeze it for up to two months.
- To reheat cooked pasta, place it in boiling water for about two minutes or microwave it for about one to two minutes.

9.3. How to Defrost Pasta

Storing and defrosting pasta properly is important to ensure its quality and taste. Here's more information on how to defrost pasta:

1. Defrosting Fresh Pasta
- Fresh pasta should be thawed in the refrigerator overnight or for at least four hours. This will help to maintain its texture and prevent it from becoming sticky.
- Once thawed, the pasta can be cooked immediately or stored in the refrigerator for up to twenty-four hours.

2. Defrosting Cooked Pasta
- To defrost cooked pasta, remove it from the freezer and place it in the refrigerator for twenty-four hours.

- If you're in a hurry, you can also microwave the cooked pasta for a few minutes, stirring occasionally, until it has fully defrosted or in a pot of warm water on the stove.
- Microwave defrosting is the quickest method, but it can cause the pasta to become overcooked or mushy. To avoid this, it is best to defrost the pasta in small portions and stir it frequently.
- Defrosting in a pot of warm water on the stove takes longer, but it helps to preserve the pasta's texture. The pot should be covered to keep the heat and moisture inside. The pasta should be stirred frequently to prevent it from sticking together.
- It is important to note that both fresh and cooked pasta can become watery or mushy after being defrosted, so it's best to use them in dishes where they will be further cooked or incorporated into sauces.

CHAPTER 10: CONCLUSION

10.1. Final Thoughts on Cooking Homemade Pasta

Cooking homemade pasta is a wonderful and satisfying experience. Not only does it allow you to control the quality and ingredients of your pasta, but it also gives you a chance to get creative with flavors and shapes. Whether you're a seasoned chef or you just started learning how to cook, making homemade pasta is a fun and rewarding endeavor.

One of the great things about homemade pasta is the flexibility it offers in terms of ingredients. You can use semolina flour for a chewy texture, or add ingredients like eggs, herbs, or spices to create unique flavors. Homemade pasta is also great for those with food allergies or special dietary requirements, as you can use alternative flours such as gluten-free or whole grain options.

When it comes to cooking homemade pasta, there are a few key steps to keep in mind. First, be sure to knead the dough well to develop the gluten and ensure the pasta will hold its shape when cooked. Then, let the dough rest for a short period of time to allow the gluten to relax and make it easier to roll and cut. When cutting the pasta, you can either use a rolling pin and knife or a pasta machine to create the desired shape.

Once the pasta is cut, it's time to cook it. Freshly made pasta takes a shorter time to cook than dried pasta, so be sure to keep a close eye on it while it's boiling. It's also important to salt the cooking water well, as this will help to enhance the flavor of the pasta. When the pasta is cooked, be sure to drain it thoroughly and then toss it with a little bit of oil or butter to prevent it from sticking together.

When it comes to freezing and storing homemade pasta, there are a few things to keep in mind. Fresh pasta can be frozen for up to two months, and it's best to freeze it on a sheet tray in a single line before transferring it to a freezer-safe bag. Cooked pasta can also be frozen, but it's important to make sure it's well-drained and cooled before freezing to prevent it from becoming mushy when defrosted.

Defrosting pasta can be done either in the refrigerator overnight or in the microwave. If using the microwave, be sure to stir the pasta every thirty seconds to ensure that it defrosts evenly. Once the pasta is defrosted, it can be reheated in a saucepan on the stove or in the microwave.

When it comes to storing pasta, fresh pasta can be preserved in the fridge for up to two days, or in the freezer for up to two months. Prepared pasta can be preserved in the fridge for up to five days, or in the freezer for up to two months. When storing cooked pasta, it's important to make sure it's well-drained and stored in an airtight container to prevent it from becoming dry and hard.

In conclusion, cooking homemade pasta is a wonderful and rewarding experience that offers many benefits. From the flexibility of ingredients to the control over flavor and texture, making your own pasta is a great way to get creative in the kitchen and enjoy a delicious meal. Whether you're a seasoned chef or you just started learning how to cook, taking the time to make your own pasta is a worthwhile endeavor. By following these steps and guidelines, you can create perfectly cooked pasta every time. Whether you're making fresh pasta or using dried pasta, the options are endless and the results are always delicious. Don't be scared to try new ideas or go overboard or experiment, such as with different shapes and sauces, to find your perfect pasta dish. And most importantly, enjoy the process and the end result. Bon appétit!

10.2. Future of Homemade Pasta

The future of homemade pasta is bright and exciting, as people are increasingly interested in cooking and eating wholesome, nutritious, and delicious food. People are becoming more and more inclined to want to make their own distinctive and delicious meals, especially pasta dishes, as a result of the emergence of foodie culture, the popularity of culinary shows, and food-related websites.

Homemade pasta is a great way to enjoy the rich flavors and textures of this classic food, while also having control over the ingredients used and the nutritional value of the meal. As people continue to become more interested in health and wellness, they are seeking out wholesome ingredients and simple recipes, and pasta is a great option to achieve these goals.

In the future, we can expect to see an increased demand for unique and creative pasta recipes, as well as new and innovative pasta-making tools and techniques. With advances in technology and cooking, it is more likely that we'll witness even more modern pasta-making machines and equipment that make the process even easier and more convenient for home cooks.

Additionally, with the rise of plant-based diets, there is a growing interest in alternative pasta ingredients, such as legumes, vegetables, and grains, which offer new and delicious ways to incorporate pasta into a healthy and sustainable diet.

Overall, the future of homemade pasta is full of opportunity and promise, and it is an exciting time for anyone who loves to cook and create their own delicious meals. Whether you're a seasoned chef or you just started learning how to cook, there is something for everyone when it comes to making and enjoying delicious, homemade pasta.

10.3. A Final Note from the Author

Dear reader,

As a passionate home cook and lover of all things pasta, I am thrilled to share this book with you. I have a deep belief that there is absolutely nothing quite like the taste and comfort of a warm bowl of homemade pasta, and I hope that this book will inspire you to try making it yourself.

I have endeavored to include a wide variety of recipes, from classic favorites to innovative new dishes, and I hope that you will find something in here that appeals to you. I have also included information on pairing pasta with wine, as well as tips on how to freeze and store your pasta for later.

I have put my heart and soul into this book, and I truly believe that it will help you to bring the joy of homemade pasta into your own kitchen. Whether you're a seasoned chef or you just started learning how to cook, I hope that you will find the recipes and information in this book to be useful and inspiring.

Thank you for choosing this book, and I wish you the very best as you begin your pasta-making journey.

Buon appetito!

Sincerely,

William Hunt

APPENDICES

11.1. Troubleshooting Guide for Common Problems

Problem: The pasta dough is too dry and crumbly.

Solution: If the pasta dough is too dry, it is likely that not enough liquid was added or that the dough was overworked during kneading. To fix this, add a small amount of water, one teaspoon at a time, until the dough comes together. Avoid overworking the dough to prevent further drying.

Problem: The pasta dough is too sticky.

Solution: If the pasta dough is too sticky, it is likely that too much liquid was added or that the dough was not floured enough during rolling. To fix this, add a small amount of flour, one teaspoon at a time, until the dough is no longer sticky. Be sure to flour your work surface and rolling pin well before rolling the dough.

Problem: The pasta is too thick or too thin.

Solution: The thickness of the pasta dough is determined by the amount of flour and liquid used, as well as the amount of rolling and stretching. If the pasta is too thick, add a small amount of water to the dough and continue to knead. If the pasta is too thin, add a small amount of flour to the dough and continue to knead.

Problem: The pasta is sticking together.

Solution: Pasta can stick together if it is not floured well or if it is overcooked. To prevent sticking, be sure to flour the pasta well before boiling and avoid overcooking by following the recommended boiling time for the specific pasta shape you are making. If the pasta is already stuck together, gently separate it with your fingers or a fork.

Problem: The pasta is overcooked or mushy.

Solution: Overcooked pasta can be caused by boiling the pasta for too long or not draining the pasta well enough after boiling. To prevent overcooking, follow the recommended boiling time for the specific pasta shape you are making and drain the pasta well before serving. If the pasta is already overcooked, try using it in a pasta salad or a baked pasta dish to help mask the texture.

Problem: Sauce not sticking to pasta.

Solution: If the sauce is not sticking to the pasta, it could be due to the pasta being too dry or the sauce being too thin. To avoid this, make sure to cook the pasta in enough boiling water, drain it well, and toss it with the sauce while still warm. You can also add a little bit of the pasta cooking water to the sauce to help it adhere to the pasta.

11.2. Conversion Charts for Ingredients

Cooking is often considered a blend of science, art, and even geography. The origin and quality of ingredients, such as flour and sugar, can vary by country and impact the final taste and texture of your dish. While we can provide conversions for weights and measures, we cannot guarantee that a recipe made in Canada or England will taste exactly the same as one made in the United States. That's why we encourage you to trust your instincts and use visual cues, like the dough coming together in a ball, to determine if you need to make adjustments.

Our recipes were developed using U.S. measurements following government guidelines, but we've included charts with U.S. and metric equivalents to help with conversions. Please note that all conversions are approximate and rounded to the nearest whole number. So go ahead, be the judge and let your taste buds guide you.

For example:
1 teaspoon = 4.9292 milliliters, rounded up to 5 milliliters

1 ounce = 28.3495 grams, rounded down to 28 grams

VOLUME CONVERSIONS

U.S.	METRIC
1 teaspoon	5 milliliters
2 teaspoons	10 milliliters
1 tablespoon	15 milliliters
2 tablespoons	30 milliliters
1/4 cup	59 milliliters
1/3 cup	79 milliliters
1/2 cup	118 milliliters
3/4 cup	177 milliliters
1 cup	237 milliliters
1 1/4 cups	296 milliliters
1 1/2 cups	355 milliliters
2 cups (1 pint)	473 milliliters
2 1/2 cups	591 milliliters
3 cups	710 milliliters
4 cups (1 quart)	40.946 liter
1.06 quarts	1 liter
4 quarts (1 gallon)	3.8 liters

WEIGHT CONVERSIONS

OUNCES	GRAMS
1/2	14
3/4	21
1	28
1 1/2	43
2	57
2 1/2	71
3	85
3 1/2	99
4	113
4 1/2	128
5	142
6	170
7	198
8	227
9	255
10	283
12	340
16 (1 pound)	454

Flour

1 cup...140g
1 tablespoon.................................9g
1 teaspoon....................................3g
1 ounce....................................28.35g
1 pound..................................453.59g

Eggs

1 large egg..................................50g
1 egg yolk...................................20g
1 egg white..................................30g

Liquid

1 cup.......................................235ml
1 tablespoon..............................15ml
1 teaspoon...................................5ml
1 quart....................................946ml

Salt

1 teaspoon....................................6g
1 tablespoon................................18g

Butter

1 cup.......................................227g
1 tablespoon................................14g
1 teaspoon.................................4.5g

Sugar

1 cup.......................................200g
1 tablespoon................................12g
1 teaspoon....................................4g

Olive Oil

1 cup.......................................220g
1 tablespoon................................14g
1 teaspoon.................................4.5g

Grated Cheese

1 cup.......................................100g
1 tablespoon..................................6g
1 teaspoon....................................2g

Note: These conversions are approximate and may vary slightly based on the density of the ingredient. It is always best to weigh ingredients for the most accurate results when cooking or baking.

OVERTHUPERATURES

FAHRENHEIT	CELSIUS
225	105
250	120
275	135
300	150
325	165
350	180
375	190
400	200
425	220
450	230
475	245

11.3. Glossary of Terms Related to Pasta Making

- Al Dente: Italian term meaning "to the tooth," referring to pasta that is cooked so that it is still firm when bitten.

-
- Durum Wheat: A type of wheat that is high in protein and gluten, commonly used in making pasta.

-
- Gluten: A protein found in wheat flour that gives pasta dough its elasticity and strength.

-
- Kneading: The process of working the pasta dough with your hands to develop the gluten and form a smooth, elastic dough.

-
- Semolina: A type of flour made from durum wheat that is coarser and higher in gluten than all-purpose flour, often used in pasta dough.

-
- Pasta Maker: A kitchen tool used to roll and cut pasta dough into various shapes.

-
- Rolling Pin: A cylindrical kitchen tool used to roll out pasta dough.

-
- Pasta drying rack: A rack used to hang pasta to dry and harden before cooking.

-
- Fresh pasta: Pasta that is made with eggs, flour, and water, and has a softer texture than dried pasta.

-
- Dried pasta: Pasta that is made with semolina flour and water, and has been dried for storage and shelf-life.

-
- Sheet: A thin layer of pasta dough used to make various pasta shapes.

-
- Resting: the process of letting pasta dough rest for a period of time, usually about thirty minutes, to allow the gluten to relax and the dough to become more pliable.

ABOUT THE AUTHOR

William Hunt was born in the heart of Tuscany, Italy, where he developed a love and appreciation for good food at a young age. His family, who had been in the restaurant business for generations, instilled in him a passion for cooking and a strong work ethic. William started cooking in his family's restaurant kitchen when he was just ten years old, and by the time he was a teenager, he was already experimenting with different recipes and ingredients.

After finishing culinary school, William worked in various kitchens across Italy, honing his skills and expanding his knowledge of traditional Italian cuisine. In his early twenties, he decided to strike out on his own and open a small trattoria in Florence. The restaurant was an instant success, attracting food lovers from all over the world who came to taste William's delectable dishes.

In his late twenties, William was offered the opportunity to bring his culinary skills to America. He moved to New York City, where he opened a highly acclaimed Italian restaurant. Over the next few years, William became a sought-after chef and a beloved figure in the New York food scene.

William's passion for cooking and teaching others has led him to write several cookbooks, including Mastering the Art of Homemade Pasta: Secrets of Delicious Fresh Pasta from Italy with Your Own Hands. In this book, William shares his love of cooking pasta and offers tips and tricks for creating authentic and delicious dishes at home. He also provides wine pairing suggestions to help readers complete the perfect meal.

When he's not in the kitchen, William enjoys traveling the world, exploring new ingredients, and taking cooking classes. He also dedicates time to various culinary charities, working to promote healthy eating and cooking habits among children. William currently resides in New York City with his wife and two children.

ABOUT US

Savory Pages Publishing is a new and exciting publishing house on Amazon that is dedicated to publishing high-quality cookbooks for food lovers and aspiring chefs alike. At Savory Pages, we believe that cooking is an art form, and we strive to provide our readers with cookbooks that are as beautiful as they are useful.

Our team of talented chefs, food writers, and editors work together to produce cookbooks that are packed with delicious recipes, stunning photography, and helpful cooking tips and techniques. We cover a wide range of cuisines and cooking styles, from classic French cuisine to modern plant-based cooking, and everything in between.

At Savory Pages, we are passionate about food, and we believe that cooking should be a joyous and fulfilling experience. That's why we focus on creating cookbooks that not only provide readers with delicious recipes but also inspire them to experiment and explore new flavors and techniques in the kitchen.

Whether you're a seasoned home cook or just starting out, we have a cookbook that is perfect for you. So come explore the world of cooking with Savory Pages Publishing, and discover a whole new world of delicious possibilities!

SHARE YOUR THOUGHTS

Dear valued reader,

At Savory Pages Publishing, we are committed to creating the best possible experience for our readers, and your feedback is critical to achieving that goal. We want to hear from you about your experience with our latest book.

If you have any suggestions, complaints or feedback you'd like to share, please don't hesitate to reach out to us at: savorypages@gmail.com. We're always looking for ways to improve our offerings, and your input can help us create better books that meet the needs of our readers.

We understand that your time is valuable, and we appreciate your willingness to share your thoughts with us. We promise to carefully consider your feedback and use it to inform our future publications.

Thank you for your support of Savory Pages Publishing. We're honored that you've chosen our book, and we look forward to hearing from you soon.

Best regards,

Savory Pages Publishing.

RECIPE LIST

Shapes and Forms of Pasta

Variations of Pasta Dough

Pasta Recipes

Agnolotti

Capellini (Angel Hair)

Conchiglie (shells)

Farfalle

Fettuccine

Fettuccine with Clam Sauce 87
Fettuccine with Mushroom Sauce 88
Fettuccine with Shrimp Scampi 88

Fusilli (spiral)
Creamy Tomato and Spinach Fusilli 162
Fusilli with Broccoli Rabe and Sausage 162
Fusilli with Pesto and Cherry Tomatoes 160
Fusilli with Spicy Tomato Sauce 160

Gnocchi
Potato Gnocchi 018
Pumpkin Gnocchi 110
Spinach Gnocchi 108
Sweet Potato Gnocchi 109
Tomato Gnocchi 110

Lasagna
Chicken Alfredo Lasagna 99
Classic Meat Lasagna 96
Seafood Lasagna 98
Spinach and Ricotta Lasagna 97

Linguine
Linguine with Clams 92
Linguine with Garlic and Oil 94
Linguine with Mussels 95
Linguine with Spinach and Ricotta 94
Linguine with Tomato and Basil Sauce 92

Orecchiette
Orecchiette with Broccoli and Garlic 153
Orecchiette with Broccoli Rabe and Sausage 152
Orecchiette with Sausage and Peppers 154
Orecchiette with Sun-Dried Tomatoes and

Spinach 152

Pappardelle
Pappardelle with Chicken and Asparagus 114
Pappardelle with Bolognese Sauce 112
Pappardelle with Mushroom Sauce 115
Pappardelle with Roasted Tomato Sauce 116
Pappardelle with Shrimp Scampi 112

Penne
Penne alla Vodka 142
Penne with Chicken and Broccoli 146
Penne with Pesto Sauce 145
Penne with Shrimp Scampi 144
Penne with Tomato and Basil Sauce 142

Ravioli
Butternut Squash Ravioli 149
Classic Cheese Ravioli 148
Mushroom and Herb Ravioli 150
Shrimp and Lobster Ravioli 150
Spinach and Ricotta Ravioli 148

Radiatori (radiator-like)
Radiatori Carbonara 167
Radiatori with Creamy Shrimp Scampi Sauce 166
Radiatori with Pesto and Roasted Vegetables 164
Radiatori with Tomato and Basil Sauce 164

Rotini
Classic Rotini Pasta Salad 172
Creamy Rotini and Chicken Bake 174
Rotini and Meatball Casserole 174
Rotini and Vegetable Stir-Fry 172

Pesto Sauce

Arugula Pesto **193**

Classic Basil Pesto **193**

Spinach Pesto **193**

Sun-Dried Tomato Pesto **193**

Walnut Pesto **193**

Puttanesca Sauce

Classic Puttanesca Sauce **196**

Puttanesca Sauce with Anchovies **196**

Puttanesca Sauce with Chicken **196**

Puttanesca Sauce with Olives and Capers **196**

Puttanesca Sauce with Shrimp **196**

Tomato Sauce

Classic Tomato Sauce **192**

Tomato Sauce with Anchovies **192**

Tomato Sauce with Fresh Basil **192**

Tomato Sauce with Mushrooms **192**

Tomato Sauce with Olives and Capers **192**

Vodka Sauce

Classic Vodka Sauce **195**

Vodka Sauce with Chicken **195**

Vodka Sauce with Shrimp **195**

Vodka Sauce with Spinach and Ricotta **195**

Vodka Sauce with Tomatoes and Basil **195**